THE NEW ASCETICISM

The New Asceticism

Sexuality, Gender and the Quest for God

Sarah Coakley

B L O O M S B U R Y

LONDON • OXFORD • NEW YORK • NEW DELHI • SYDNEY

Bloomsbury Continuum
An imprint of Bloomsbury Publishing Plc

50 Bedford Square   1385 Broadway
London wc1b 3dp   New York, NY 10018
UK   USA

www.bloomsbury.com

Bloomsbury, Continuum and the Diana logo are trademarks of Bloomsbury
Publishing Plc

First published 2015

British Library Cataloguing-in-Publication Data
A catalogue record for this book is available from the British Library.

Library of Congress Cataloguing-in-Publication data has been applied for.

ISBN:
PB: 9781441103222
ePDF: 9781441173379
ePub: 9781441162243

4 6 8 10 9 7 5

Printed and bound in Great Britain by
CPI Group (UK) Ltd, Croydon cro 4yy

To find out more about our authors and books visit www.bloomsbury.com.
Here you will find extracts, author interviews, details of forthcoming events
and the option to sign up for our newsletters.

For my mother, the teacher,
who taught me to pray

And my father, the lawyer,
who taught me there is no justice
without mercy

CONTENTS

PREFACE

I OWE A GREAT DEBT OF GRATITUDE TO ROBIN BAIRD-Smith at Bloomsbury, whose idea this little book originally was, and without whose encouragement, patience and enduring goodwill I would not have brought it to completion. It was Robin who first saw that the essays I had been writing here and there in the last decade on the topics of desire and asceticism made up a consistent theme, and that this might be worthy of presentation to a wider public, indeed that its specifically Anglican origins might also have wider ecumenical interest. His understandable frustration at my many delays has been matched by a graciousness for which I want to give public thanks.

A number of my colleagues, friends, parishioners and students in both the United States and Britain have contributed their wisdom, insight and assistance to the contents of this volume. In particular I want to mention Philip McCosker, Raphael Cadenhead, David Grumett, Kimberley Patton, Charles Hefling, Columba Stewart, OSB, Truman Welch and the people of the Church of the Good Shepherd, Waban, MA, and the Brothers of the Society of St John the Evangelist at Memorial Drive, Cambridge, MA, especially Geoffrey Tristram, SSJE, Curtis Almquist, SSJE and David Vryhof, SSJE. I think they will all know why I need to thank them, and for many different blessings.

My husband Chip Coakley has conducted a fine printer's

experiment for the purposes of this book, by designing in InDesign the layout of all the pages, utilizing the lovely Gill typeface, Perpetua. This proved to be a more complex and exacting task than he had anticipated, and as ever I am indebted to him for his love and sacrificial commitment to the projects of others.

In the time in which I have been completing the editing of these essays, my parents have been painfully confronting their own ill-health, vulnerability and physical decline, after a triumphantly long marriage of over sixty-five years. Gregory of Nyssa (who features so significantly in the opening to this book) has well commented that old age and approaching death mark the boundaries in which we can best assess the meaning of desire and the project of an ascetic life; and this is as true for those who minister to, and watch with, the dying as for those who do the harder task of enduring it. I dedicate this little volume to my beloved parents as they confront this 'last battle' that leads into Life.

Sarah Coakley
Ely, Petertide, 2015

INTRODUCTION:
THE NEW ASCETICISM

THIS BOOK HAS BEEN WRITTEN IN THE CONVICTION that contemporary Western secular concerns about bodily life in general, and about 'sexuality', 'gender' and 'orientation' more specifically, are marked by certain striking and unresolved paradoxes, ones which are arguably still haunted by a lost religious past.[1] It is time therefore, this book argues, to reconsider some creative elements in that

---

1. In an earlier book, ed. Sarah Coakley, *Religion and the Body* (Cambridge: Cambridge University Press, 1997), 'Introduction: Religion and the Body', p1–10, I began to outline some of these notable contemporary paradoxes and their relation to a religious past, especially the surprising endurance of the modern philosophical ('Cartesian') idea of a distinct locus of selfhood (the intentional 'I') in some directive, or interactive, relation to the 'body'. Whilst anti-dualistic 'physicalism' and 'naturalism' have dominated in Western secular philosophy and science in the 'post-modern' period, they have held strangely little sway in the cultural world of slimming magazines and body-building, where control of the 'body' from some other site of surveillance (the 'I') is still taken as read. This might be said to be the *dominating* 'paradox' of bodiliness in the privileged post-modern West: does reductive scientific physicalism really reign, or does a stark dualism still dominate our obsessions with manufactured fitness and sexual youthfulness? Yet the very notion of 'body' across the major religious traditions is much more ambiguous and labile than these two 'secularized' alternatives suggest, as *Religion and the Body* goes on to chart. In short, one can assume no shared and unambiguous meaning in the notion of 'body' today in the 'multi-cultural' West, only perhaps the presumption that the sphere of personal materiality is one in which some battle of personal 'salvation' is to be won or lost.

religious past, ones which may have been repeatedly suppressed or misunderstood in recent decades. But this task of critical retrieval is not easy, and involves a necessary preamble to identify why the topic of 'sexuality' has become such a paroxysmic and emotive subject in contemporary discussion. Since it is easy to swim unthinkingly in the tide of prevailing cultural obsessions, it is often, by the same token, surprisingly difficult to identify the hidden currents which are pulling those debates in opposing directions. The churches, moreover, are by no means immune from such conflicting 'secular' undertows. Indeed often it is within the churches (and particularly within the established church, if a country has one) that such pervasive cultural anxieties are played out with special force: an established church, however depleted numerically, may become the symbolic locus of discussion for a more general unresolved cultural dilemma.[2]

Hence the current ecclesiastical furores about 'sexuality' may *seem* strange, even repulsive, to a watching 'secular' world-without-religion.[3] But in fact, as I argue in the essays

2. This is a repeated theme in the recent work of the British sociologist of religion, Grace Davie. See for instance her chapter 'Debate', in eds Samuel Wells and Sarah Coakley, *Praying for England: Priestly Presence in Contemporary Culture* (London: Continuum, 2008), pp. 147–69.

3. I use the term 'secular' in this Introduction with some hesitation, fully aware that those who are not institutional religious *practitioners* may nonetheless harbour considerable interests in 'spiritual' and 'religious' topics: see Charles Taylor's *A Secular Age* (Cambridge, MA: Harvard University Press, 2007), pp. 1–22, who reflects with insight on the paradoxical sense of religious 'optionality' in contemporary Western 'secularism'. Yet, by reverse logic, those within the churches are also subject,

gathered in this volume, they are the working out of a co-nundrum about desire and gratification in both the Christian tradition and the contemporary secular West (which is so much its own product). And they encode both the worst in the Christian tradition (abuse, denial, duplicity, patriarchal dominance, arrogant refusal to listen to feminist and gay voices), and something of the best (a longing for sexual justice, for family and social stability, for a world in which pleasure and commitment are rightly related, for a loving realism about sexual frailty and forgiveness worthy of the teaching of Jesus, its founder).

Yet it is an unfortunate but predictable feature of the current 'homosexuality' debates, specifically, that it is the extreme positions (both within and outside the churches) which are the ones which get all the attention. These extremes are also widely and straightforwardly associated, at least in the press, with *political* as well as theological 'conservatism' and 'liberalism', an analysis which oversimplifies a much more complicated set of alternatives in reality. This unfortunate state of affairs effectively obliterates the possibility of a discussion which would move the debate beyond 'repression' and its seeming opposite – promiscuous libertinism. Thus a much bigger challenge has here been missed: that of how to evaluate and *adjudicate* desires, both sexual and others, and how to live a life of balance and moderation

often unconsciously and subliminally, to cultural forces and interests propelled by anti-religious *animus*. In short, the line between 'religious' and 'secular' is blurred and complicated in current Western mores, and nowhere more than in the realm of the 'sexual' is this apparent.

such that desire is negotiated with ascetical realism, and in a mode conducive to genuine human flourishing. And this is a challenge whose significance clearly spreads well beyond the Christian fold. Moreover (and as a little further reflection begins to make obvious), this is also a matter that affects not just individuals, but families, societies and political and economic realities world-wide.

At the heart of this book, then, is an analysis of a striking contemporary confusion about 'desire' itself, a clarification of the unconscious paradoxes that inhere in this confusion, and a proposal for its resolution through the recovery of a new vision of 'ascetic' life. Clearly both these key terms ('desire', 'asceticism') require careful definition. The first purpose of this book, then, is to suggest a new way of defining and thinking about these two topics and their relation: this project animates the volume as a whole, and is repeatedly returned to throughout it. The chief problem with the category of 'desire' is that it has become so heavily sexualized in the modern, post-Freudian period as to render its connection with other desires (including the desire for God) obscure and puzzling. The chief problem with the category of 'asceticism' is that within the same period it has become larded with the negative associations of repression, ecclesiastical authoritarianism, and denial. It follows that another, and deeper, level of reflection is required if these difficulties are to be faced and resolved.

The second purpose of this book therefore unfolds from here. It is to suggest a means of resolution of these entangled problems, one which is unambiguously and unashamedly *theological*. This second proposal constitutes the theological heart of the chapters that follow: that the nature of desire, for all its notable and conflicting philosophical theorizations in contemporary secular life, fundamentally requires prior theological analysis if its full implications for human flourishing are to be understood.[4] Once these two central convictions in the book are creatively in play (the necessary connection of desire and asceticism, and the necessarily theological rendition of this same nexus), the spiritual and ethical idea of 'the new asceticism' begins to take shape. The core argument that is mounted though the various essays gathered here is that only a revived, purged – and lived – form of 'ascetic' life will rescue the churches from their current theological divisions and incoherences over 'sexuality'; and only the same authentically 'ascetic' life will be demanding enough to command the respect of a post-Christian world saturated and sated by the commodi-

---

4. I make this case in more depth and with much more extensive historical illustration, in the first volume of my systematic theology, *God, Sexuality and the Self: An Essay 'On the Trinity'* (Cambridge: Cambridge University Press, 2013). The argument involves a fresh acknowledgement of the creative elision of biblical and Platonic ideas about desire that occurred in the early Christian centuries: Yahweh's primal desire for Israel/Church and the soul's responsive desire for God (as celebrated in the prophetic books, the psalms and the Song of Songs) was there fused with Plato's idea of human desire (as always intrinsically tugged back to the heavenly realm of the 'forms'). On this view, desire is 'the constellating category of selfhood, the ineradicable root of one's longing for God' (ibid, 26, 58). The contrapuntal (and complementary) relation of *God, Sexuality and the Self* with the essays gathered in this book is remarked upon at several points, *intra*.

fications of desire. When the ascetic life works, and works well, it unifies, intensifies and ultimately purifies desire in the crucible of divine love, paradoxically imparting true freedom precisely by the narrowing of choices. If this is where 'true joys are to be found' then the lost theological wisdom of the ascetic life is indeed one worth retrieving.

But where are we to start in this project of retrieval? Our very understanding of 'desire' is the first hurdle to be negotiated.

Retrieving 'Desire' from 'Sex'

Gregory of Nyssa, the fourth-century Greek theologian who features large in this volume, had the (to us) strange insight that desire relates crucially to what might be called the 'glue' of society. The 'erotic' desire that initially draws partners together sexually has also to last long enough, and to be so refined in God, as to render back to society what originally gave those partners the possibility of mutual joy: that means (beyond the immediate project of child-rearing and family) service to the poor and the outcast, attention to the frail and the orphans, a consideration of the fruit of the earth and its limitations, a vision of the whole in which all play their part, both sacrificially and joyously. It may seem odd now to say that that is where *eros* should tend; for we have so much individualized and physicalized desire that we assume that sexual enactment somehow exhausts it (and so threatens to run out completely in old age, as bodily strength withers). Thus it is the complete intertwinement of physical and *spiritual* in desire that first has to be acknowledged afresh, as well as its moral and 'eschatological' goals, if we are to reverse the modern shrinkage of thought about desire. It is noteworthy that Gregory of Nyssa also tells us that desire (properly understood) needs to be intensified (in God), never constrained or dampened, and this applies to all stages of personal life. He was, of course, operating with a mixture of Platonic thought on *eros* and his own specifically Christian insights on the rich implications of the incarnation for the possibility of transforming the body and its passions; and his is a wisdom that this book particularly urges for contemporary reconsideration.[5]

---

5. Gregory's distinctive insights on the ascetic Christian life run from his remarkable earliest text: 'On Virginity', trans. William Moore, in *Nicene and Post-Nicene Fathers of the Christian Church*, Second Series, vol. 5 (Peabody, MA: Hendrickson, 1995), pp. 343–71, up to his last great commentary on the Song of Songs: ed. and trans. Richard A. Norris, Jr., *Gregory of Nyssa: Homilies on the Song of Songs* (Atlanta: Society of Biblical Literature Press, 2013). To treat all the twists and turns in the development of Nyssen's views on the ascetic life is a complex task, since he is no systematician: the most complete treatment to date is that of Raphael Cadenhead, 'Corporeality and Desire: A Diachronic Study of Gregory of Nyssa's Ascetical Theology', Ph.D. dissertation, University of Cambridge, 2013, who comments insightfully on earlier secondary treatments. Throughout his work Gregory is effecting a new creative *rapprochement* between Plato's views on *eros* and biblical teaching on love and desire; he follows here in the tradition of Origen and the early desert fathers, parallels the profound reflections on the passions of his contemporary Evagrius of Pontus, and pre-figures others in this broad swathe of Christian Platonic tradition, particularly ps-Dionysius the Areopagite and his various inheritors in the West, including the sixteenth-century Carmelites. Chs 1, 3 and 4 in this volume variously take up themes from these authors and re-apply them to contemporary concerns.

To re-engage the insights of Gregory and those like him, however, several cultural resistances have to be overcome, and other questions and challenges addressed.

1. 'Erotic' desire has to be seen as in a tether of connected desires: for food, drink, comfort, intimacy, acknowledgement, power, pleasure, money, relaxation, rest, etc., as well as physical sex; and it must be realized that confusion, sin or excess in any one of these areas will tend inexorably to cause trouble in the others.

2. The ancient Greek challenge of *'nothing in excess'* (μηδὲν ἄγαν) has thus again to be faced: 'it is all a question of proportion' where desires are concerned, as Gregory of Nyssa puts it, and right balance is the great *desideratum* that constantly eludes us.

3. A deeper, underlying (and metaphysical) question about *eros* has also to be acknowledged: where are *true* joys to be found? Do all desires find their origin and goal in *God*, or is there any other legitimate source or end for them?

4. The answer to this conundrum cannot just be individualistic: the response – whatever is chosen, or chosen for us – is going to affect everyone we come in contact with, and so the wider society.

5. Since luck, privilege, social power and other factors seemingly cause some people to flourish more easily and others to be radically dispossessed, the further question then presses: what is the fate of *eros* when considered publicly, nationally, or globally, and how are resources to be shared?

Answers to any of these complex questions will be stretched out diachronically, both individually and culturally: there are 'long hauls' to consider, certainly longer than any modern democratically elected government of four years or so, and at least as long as any personal life-time. 'Erotic' choices in this wider sense were for Gregory and his generation tied up with the development of early monasticism into the cities, the rejection of inherited social privilege, and the relief of the urban poor and sick. They are deeply involved today, by extension, in any global planning for the tackling of disease and poverty, any response to the arms race or to sex slavery, any consideration of global warming and the threat of ecological disaster. But they *start* with individual responses to the blandishments of desire in all its forms.

Of course, much of the manipulation of our desires is effected unconsciously (and we owe it to Freud and his heirs to give insightful modern psychoanalytic accounts of how this can be so, whereas the ancient world discoursed with equal insight on the assaults of the demons of negative 'passion'). Such manipulations are diffuse, permeating socially constructed longings of which we are barely conscious but which disturbingly exercise our wills and imaginations. These *include* the desire to dominate, to subjugate, to consume and own, and to control – sexually, racially and in other ways. We need only consider the pervasive effects in Western society of advertisement, on the one hand, and pornography, on the other, to know that this must be so. Yet desire also animates good instincts and longings – to love and justice, empathy and altruism, a concern for the common good. Within this confusing mix of good and bad propulsions are clearly toxic desires that have to be brought to the light of day. But how, exactly, can that happen, if not by a systematic acknowledgement of *sin* in all its viciousness and subtlety? We tend now to prefer secular analogues such as 'addiction' or 'abuse'; but the underlying issue of the distortion and corruption of desire is what remains fundamentally at stake.

Yet, on the other side, and with a profound allure that is hard completely to suppress or deny even within a 'secular' society, desire is no less that which continuously animates us to God, as Gregory of Nyssa also taught:[6] it allures us, liberates us, gives us the energy and ecstasy of participation in the divine life, makes us humans 'fully alive' for whom nothing in the created world – as also in the divine compassion – can be 'alienated' from the same God of love.

The challenge is thus how to identify the *difference* in these many desires and how to move from the corrupt to the sublime within them – by processes of formation, self-knowledge, humility and (of course, from the perspective of Christian theology) progressive reliance on divine grace. It is here that considerations of 'habit' and 'practice' inevitably come into play in the pursuit of the virtue of a life of balanced and right-directed desire. In short, we arrive at the unavoidable realm of the 'ascetic' life.

Asceticism Under Critique: The Modern 'Exposé'

But 'asceticism' is another word, like 'desire', seemingly

---

6. The classic modern treatment of the 'endlessness' of desire in Nyssen remains Jean Daniélou, *Platonisme et Théologie Mystique* (Paris: Aubier, 1944), although it has not passed without more recent critique.

almost doomed by its modern associations. And this is what
– initially at least – makes it so hard to effect its return to
serious cultural consideration. Some of the greatest modern
cultural critics of Christianity have turned 'asceticism' back
against the tradition with ferocious and artful force. For instance, a post-Christian cultural commentator as astute as
the French philosopher and social scientist Michel Foucault
(1926–84) was entirely happy to acknowledge the intense
entanglement of (sexual) 'desire' and 'asceticism' (the first
key issue for discussion in this book, identified above); but
Foucault's definition of terms, his diagnosis of the problems
involved, and his 'genealogical' interpretation of how we
got to where we are now from a complex Christian history,
are entirely different from that which I am proposing in
this volume.[7] For Foucault, it is fundamentally a story of
power that is told in the history of 'sexuality' and attempted
ecclesiastical control of it, not a story of *God;* that theoretic
shift bespeaks likewise a secularizing of the category of desire that has deep roots both in Nietzsche's famous critique
of 'asceticism'[8] and in Freud's psychoanalytic de-throne-

---

7. See especially Michel Foucault, *The History of Sexuality* vol. 1 (London: Penguin, 1978), pp. 3–49, for Foucault's enunciation of his prime
methodological principles about sexuality and power.

8. See ed. Keith Ansell-Pearson, *Nietzsche On the Genealogy of Morality*
(Cambridge: Cambridge University Press, 2007), pp. 68–120: 'Third Essay: What Do Ascetic Ideals Mean?' For an astute analysis of Nietzsche's
account of asceticism as a pathological form of will to power, see Ty-
ler T. Roberts, ' "This Art of Transfiguration *Is* Philosophy": Nietzsche's
Asceticism', *Journal of Religion* 76 (1996), 402–27.

ment of the God-concept.[9] Once the focus moves from an intra-Christian *theological* account to a reductive hermeneutics of suspicion in relation to ascetic practice, then there simply is nothing other than power at stake: the raw physiological power of sexual *libido*, and the repressive power of churches to manage and control it. Moreover, the presumed dialectical alternative is obvious, on this rendition: if repression is the problem, then genealogical exposure and liberation from restrictive ecclesiastical *mores* constitute the only answers. The sexual repression/libertinism binary is then up and running. Much of this book is devoted to arguing that those two alternatives represent a false choice.

Yet no-one can write about sex and asceticism after Freud and Foucault without taking their probing and disturbing insights into account. Freud's account of the sexual 'unconscious', and Foucault's rendition of a certain kind of dark ecclesiastical sexual 'control', remain abiding and revealing achievements of modern critical analysis, however open to question in their fundamental a-theological assumptions. And both of these writers are more complex, subtle and volatile than any thumbnail sketch such as I have just essayed can capture. Freud, as I argue at some length in ch. 1 of this volume, changed his mind repeatedly throughout his career about the nature of sexual desire, and ended with a position curiously reminiscent of the Platonism he had apparently

---

9. For his seminal early psychoanalytic work, see Sigmund Freud, *The Interpretation of Dreams*, ed. Ritchie Robertson, trans. Joyce Crick (Oxford: Oxford University Press, 1999 [1900]), and see the discussion of Freud in ch. 1 below.

long eschewed.[10] Foucault, in contrast, was never tempted back to an *ontological* vision of desire such as one important strand of Christian thought exemplified, after Plato;[11] but in his later work Foucault radically adjusted his earlier notion of societal or ecclesiastical power to allow for a genuine individual capacity for resistant freedom and agency.[12] It follows that a careful *distinction* between (true) 'asceticism' and (false) 'repression' is the crucial and necessary one in response to Foucault's unforgettable analysis of the power of the confessional spelled out at the start of his *History of Sexuality*[13]. Foucault had aimed to show there how a particular construction of desire in the modern world is a product of institutionalized Christianity (gone awry), and thus the undertaking of a manipulative and repressive power. But is that the end of the story, we must riposte, if (as Foucault himself came to stress) the remarkable and irreducible *agency* of the human person is taken into account – its plasticity, resistance and capacity for creative transformation, including erotic transformation in relation to God? Foucault was of course right about the complicated *nexus* of power, sex and

10. See ch. 1, pp. 38–44, *intra*.

11. As in Pseudo-Dionysius, *The Divine Names*, 4,1–16, in *Pseudo-Dionysius: The Complete Works*, trans. Colm Luibheid (London: SPCK, 1987), pp. 71–83, where Dionysius famously ontologizes desire as characterizing the divine being itself. I discuss this important passage briefly in ch. 3, *intra*.

12. See especially Michel Foucault, *Power/Knowledge: Selected Interviews and Writings, 1972–1977* (New York: Pantheon Books, 1980).

13. Foucault, *The History of Sexuality*, vol. 1, esp. pp. 17–25.

selfhood – and significantly changed his own mind over time about the latter (human agency), to allow precisely for creative and shifting human resistances to political power. But by ruling out the *transcendent* agential category of 'God' in advance, he skewed the fundamental options: there was by definition no ultimate metaphysical sustainer and guarantor of *true* human freedom for Foucault, only endless negotiations and re-negotiations of human power and desire. By the same token, if power remains the central and sole organizing human category, especially in relation to an individual's 'knowledge', how can a *fully* effective ethical or epistemological critique ever be mounted against a pervasively repressive regime, even from Foucault's later methodological perspective?[14] If power merely breeds and sustains power, what can be the alternative means of redress?

In short, some of the great a-theological thinkers of the modern period (Nietzsche, Foucault, Freud) inveighed against 'asceticism' in its classic Christian forms, and made penetrating critiques of its aberrant and sometimes damaging manifestations in modern Roman Catholicism in particular. Yet, perhaps surprisingly, Freud found himself having to replace the notion of asceticism with his own (shifting) psychoanalytic account of 'sublimation'; and even Foucault did not succeed in obliterating cultural interest in the topic of asceticism. On the contrary, one might say that he unwittingly intensified that interest. Let us now explain

---

14. This point is made with particular sophistication in Miranda Fricker, *Epistemic Injustice: Power and the Ethics of Knowing* (Oxford: Oxford University Press, 2007), pp. 2–3.

how, for this takes us close to the heart of the paradoxes of desire in the contemporary West.

The Ironic Post-Modern Fascination with Extreme Asceticism

One of the more unexpected outcomes of the modern critique of Christian asceticism in the post-Nietzschean era, then, was an intoxicating new scholarly fascination, beginning from the early 1970s, with the ancient Christian forms of ascetic practice which had spawned influential models of moral formation in the late antique world. We cannot put this development down to influence from Foucault initially, since parallel intellectual developments were happening simultaneously in France, Britain and the United States: it was part of the then *Zeitgeist* (which in some ways still endures in the social sciences) and which made for an almost-obsessive interest in questions of 'bodiliness', both personal and social. It was as if the pervasive loss of belief in the 'soul' caused an intense and anxious fascination with bodiliness as the sole remaining locus of salvation.[15] In particular, second- and third-generation Freudianism was making its impact felt on an exciting new interdisciplinary historiographical development spear-headed by the British historian Peter Brown and his followers.[16] The trajec-

15. I discuss this phenomenon in more detail in my 'Introduction: Religion and the Body', in *Religion and the Body*, pp. 1–10.

16. Peter Brown's earliest, and justly celebrated, articles on 'the holy man' appeared over 40 years ago now: see esp. idem, 'The Rise and Function of the Holy Man in Late Antiquity', *The Journal of Roman Studies* 61 (1971), 80-101, which began to enunciate a theory of how ascetic holiness could manifest political power. *The World of Late Antiquity:*

tory of 'late antiquity' (Brown's coinage) became the new and expanded historical horizon for scholars frustrated by old-style clerical 'patristic' study, which had been primarily concerned with the historic development of doctrinal 'orthodoxy' and thus constrained by the periodization of the church councils. In contrast, the phenomenon of 'asceticism' in the early Christian imperial world now became newly fascinating to an emerging cadre of secularized 'scholars of religion' – again, precisely as a negotiation of ecclesial or imperial *power* rather than one of theological rectitude. Whereas the older textbooks of 'doctrine' had virtually ignored bodily ascetic practice, implicitly downgrading it to an eccentric addendum in the lives of some of the greatest early theological *thinkers*, the new students of 'late antiquity' swung the pendulum the other way, concentrating instead on the psychic, physical and political manifestations of ascetic *power* which accompanied theological debate. Indeed, there was something particularly tantalizing and paradoxical about the excitement evidenced over the more *extreme* manifestations of bodily asceticism in this rich phase of late twentieth-century scholarship; as Foucault's influence too was woven into the picture, so 'sexuality', 'gender' and 'orientation' (all modern terms and notions, of course) came to be contrapuntal tools of analysis in the examination of the late antique ascetical world.[17] Much insight was thereby to

A. D. 150-750 (New York: W. W. Norton & Company, 1971) appeared at about the same time, and set forth Brown's new periodization of the 'late antique', which cut across previous historiographic models focused on theological watersheds.

17. A good example of these scholarly traits is to be found in the

be gained: the best studies were to question the apparently unassailable modern categories of 'sexuality' that their very subjects of investigation seemed to cast into question. The sexual 'binaries' of the modern world simply did not map easily onto the extraordinary physical/spiritual subtleties and complexities of late antique ascetic life. For this reason, the more extreme this asceticism was, the more enticing it seemed – that is, the more transgressive of, and releasing from, settled *modern* Christian mores and teachings, especially on 'sexuality'.[18] Yet – and herein lies the chief paradox exemplified in this methodological novelty – the more suggestive its extremism, the less likely that its own demanding 'asceticism', as such, would be proposed as a *working* contemporary option. Late antique 'gender fluidity', so called, could be co-opted for a delicious post-modern movement for sexual liberation (especially 'homosexual', 'bi-sexual' or 'trans-sexual' liberation); but these liberations would be altogether devoid of the hard-graft ascetic denial that had originally spawned it. This was, as one ex-Jesuit late-antique scholar acutely remarked, a form of 'armchair asceticism',[19]

volume dedicated to Elizabeth A. Clark (herself an outstanding mentor and exemplar of these trends): eds Dale B. Martin and Patricia Cox Miller, *The Cultural Turn in Late Antique Studies: Gender, Asceticism and Historiography* (Durham, NC: Duke University Press, 2005).

18. A controversial example of such a method is to be found in Virginia Burrus, *'Begotten, Not Made': Conceiving Manhood in Late Antiquity* (Stanford: Stanford University Press, 2000), whose reading of Gregory of Nyssa differs markedly from my own.

19. This delicious phrase is consistently attributed to Philip Rousseau of the Catholic University of America, but I have been unable to trace a precise reference. See however Gillian Clark, *Christianity and Roman*

titillated intellectually by antique ascetic rigour, but for the most part quite unthinkingly accommodated to post-modern self-indulgence. Asceticism had become voyeuristic, something to study but not actually to *do*.

Asceticism, Good and Bad

However, even this was not the whole picture, or the last word. A minority report from philosophers and theologians creatively influenced by the new 'late antique' paradigm was also to emerge in its wake. Indeed, the critique of Foucault by his contemporary Parisian interlocutor, the ancient philosopher Pierre Hadot, had already focused the issue between them on how philosophy and 'spiritual practice' needed to be thought of as integrally *combined* in any ethic worthy of its late antique ancestry:[20] to propound the theory without the practice was a charade, a *chimera*. Some astute theologians with monastic formation now also made the same point: ascetic formation, properly understood, involves a demanding integration of intellectual, spiritual and bodily practice over a life-time, sustained by a complete vision of the Christian life and its 'ends'. To speak of an 'ascetic impulse', therefore, as one important long-term research project in late antiquity did in the early 1990s, was to beg crucial questions about whether 'impulses' were likely

Society (Cambridge: Cambridge University Press, 2004), p. 69, who makes the same attribution.

20. See especially Pierre Hadot's celebrated essays on the integration of 'spiritual exercises' and ancient philosophy: ed. Arnold Davidson, *Philosophy as a Way of Life: Spiritual Exercises from Socrates to Foucault* (Oxford: Blackwell, 1995).

to *lead* to 'ascetic practices' or more likely to need checking by them.[21] Thus, as one strand of development from the new fascination with late antique asceticism issued in liberationist moves for alternative forms of sexual expression, another sprang up which returned to the serious moral demands of monastic life-forms and their contemporary personal and political significance.[22] It is this latter strand of thought that is developed in this book, one that becomes particularly *à propos*, I argue, in the wake of numerous clerical sex scandals and of the deeply disunifying ecclesial effect of arguments about human (homo)sexuality.

The Paradoxes of Desire and Asceticism

It is clear, therefore, as mentioned at the start of this

---

21. The 'ascetic impulse' was a group scholarly project spear-headed by Vincent L. Wimbush, which held meetings at the American Academy of Religion and a major conference in 1993, producing eds Vincent L. Wimbush and Richard Valantasis, *Asceticism* (New York: Oxford University Press, 1995). See the probing and critical review by Columba Stewart, OSB, 'Asceticism and Spirituality in Late Antiquity: New Vision, Impasse or Hiatus', in *Christian Spirituality Bulletin* 4 (1996), 11–17, which impenitently, but charitably, underscores the methodological confusion in the volume and the underlying resistance to theological and spiritual realities.

22. The latter trend may be variously seen at work in (e.g.) Columba Stewart's own richly theological study of *Cassian the Monk* (New York: Oxford University Press, 1998); and — rather differently — in Alasdair MacIntyre's famous philosophical retrieval of the Benedictine Rule, at the close of his *After Virtue: A Study in Moral Theory* (Notre Dame, IN: University of Notre Dame Press, 1981), as an antidote to post-modern ethical relativism and rootlessness. (For more on MacIntyre on Benedict and 'practices' of virtue, see ch. 4, *intra*.)

Introduction, that the central topics of desire and asceticism discussed in this book are offered at a period of extreme divergence and confusion about their meaning, relation and significance. In particular, we are now in a position to see that a number of overlapping cultural paradoxes afflicts any attempts to deal with them straightforwardly; and at the same time this tension tends implicitly to block or resist any attempts at *theological* resolution. It is perhaps worth enumerating these paradoxes more clearly at this point, since much that follows in this book is an attempt at moving beyond them, resolving them moreover in a way that necessarily brings God into the picture as the source and goal of all human desire.

We noted, first,[23] how strangely paradoxical are the different approaches to bodiliness that permeate contemporary Western scientific and medical investigation on the one hand, and cultural investment in bodily 'control' and maximization of health on the other. Whilst we have been living through a long phase of regnant physicalism and reductionism in philosophy of mind in the academy,[24] and a parallel intensification of the detached medical/clinical ap-

---

23. In note 1, above.

24. One example of a fine textbook in philosophy of mind from the 1990s that reflected that dominating physicalist trend, and which I have often used in teaching, is eds Richard Warner and Tadeusz Szubka, *The Mind-Body Problem* (Oxford: Blackwell, 1994). It must be said that the last few years have evidenced a shift towards much greater acceptance of forms of dualism in philosophy of mind, especially 'dual aspect' theories (as opposed to Cartesian 'substance dualism', though that too has its followers).

proach to the body which has recently been dubbed that of an 'anticipatory corpse',[25] one would never guess any of this from a reading of popular sports, diet and health magazines, where the quest for personal 'control' over resistant 'flesh' resummons a dualism at least as strong as that of Descartes. In short, questions of 'desire' and 'asceticism' attach to this primary paradox and implicitly force some sort of decision: *is* human selfhood *nothing but* fleshly physicality, genetically coded in particular ways and thus to a large extent determined in its 'choice' and action? Or do 'I' have a conscious existence and freedom that is at least distinguishable in some significant way from my neurophysiological bodily manifestations, and in whom 'desire' rises to a level beyond the satisfaction of mere physical needs to higher spiritual and cultural aspirations? A lot hangs on the resolution of this first paradox.

A second paradox, however, already discussed at some length above, seemingly nestles within the first. That is: is bodily sexual desire, in particular, a phenomenon which *demands* physical satisfaction, such that its denial would not only potentially threaten sanity but represent a refusal of a fundamental human 'right to happiness'? Or is some necessary restraint required if law, order and cultural stability are to endure? Again, we see both propulsions of thought constantly manifested in the newspapers and popular discussion, seemingly without any sense of paradoxical strain.

---

25. See Jeffrey Bishop's much-discussed book, *The Anticipatory Corpse: Medicine, Power and the Care of the Dying* (Notre Dame, IN: Notre Dame University Press, 2011).

On the one hand, sexual pleasure is a 'private' matter – a 'right' which is unquestionably accepted as unproblematic and even somehow necessary in its activation; on the other hand it is rapidly condemned when *certain forms* of excess or aberration become manifestly harmful, whereupon prurient and violent condemnation follows.[26] But perhaps, as we have intimated above, the picture is yet more complex and subtle, such that 'ascetic rigour' can in some circumstances not only 'sublimate' sexual desire but itself represent an enticing (even 'sexy'!) alternative, one that precisely attracts the attention of the post-modern scholar of late antiquity for its zaniness, its resistance of normalcy, its power to change the 'rules' of society? If so, then the same paradoxicality may just repeat itself at a new level, leading to a libertine interpretation of late antique 'gender fluidity' on the one hand, and a weirdly voyeuristic but distanced fascination on the other.

A parallel oddity (and third paradox) is to be found in the arena of food and drink, where craven self-indulgence, constantly encouraged through advertisement and its allure, sits alongside self-punitive sports and dieting (e.g., the current

---

26. As a characteristic headline in the *Guardian* help pages recently ran: 'you have a right [*sic*] to any sexual pleasure you want ... providing it doesn't break the law'. The question that then immediately presses is: what if you have desires that intrinsically 'break the law'? How can this libertinistic approach supply any insight into how to keep (just) the right side of the law? I discuss some further confusions and sub-paradoxes that arise from this basic tension between 'rights', freedom and the social good in relation to both heterosexual and homosexual sexuality in ch. 1, *intra*.

5/2 craze[27]), with one extreme often ricocheting into the other. As one journalist has recently commented: 'intermittent fasting suits the modern mindset — [on account of] its *narcissistic* combination of self-denial and gratification.'[28] This pithy headline well expresses our third paradox: fasting can itself become indulgent. Yet there is little, if any, discussion in the cultural media of how excess and loss of control in one area of 'desire' may have implications for other areas: rarely, if ever, does one hear criticism of obesity in the clergy, for instance (a common problem under the stresses of clerical life); and never is it commented that loss of control in fasting (from food or alcohol) might be connected with loss of sexual continence amidst the ranks of the celibate. This is particularly odd given the profound insights on this point made not only in the New Testament by Paul (in his dealings with the multiply divisive problems in the church at Corinth)[29], and in a long tradition of wisdom on

---

27. That is, fasting for two days each week.

28. Louise France, 'Eat what you like: the science that has overturned the diet industry', *The Times* colour supplement, Saturday, 4 January 2014, p. 25 (my emphasis).

29. See especially 1 Cor. chs 5–11, which are variously concerned with sexual matters and questions of food and drink, and which climax in Paul's theology of the balanced, inter-dependent 'mystical body' in ch. 12. It is significant that in the Pauline and deutero-Pauline letters there is equal concern with both licentiousness and extreme or misdirected asceticism (see too Col. 2.16–23); the fine line between false control (what would later be called a 'Pelagian' sensibility) and true ascetic 'loss of control' in God is what is at stake (see Paul's pithy remark in 2 Cor. 5.13: the goal is to be 'out of one's mind' for *God*, but 'sober' in the human realm). That is why, already for Paul, 'God' is clearly more

bodily passions in early monastic writing (especially in the great synthesizers of that tradition, Evagrius and Cassian).[30] Perhaps, as prayer atrophies under the stresses and evasions of an unbalanced clerical life, theological resources such as these become ever more remote to consciousness.

In sum, the strain evidenced in these cultural paradoxes is perhaps more obvious in their resultant epiphenomena than in any explicit clarity in enunciating them. But these accompanying signs of dis-ease are arguably themselves an indication that a distinctly modern, physicalist paradigm of bodiliness (reductive, deterministic, often hedonist) is cracking and shifting – that the realm of the 'body' is being re-drawn not only personally but politically. And certainly there are already plenty of indications in the so-called 'secular' world that 'asceticism' of some sort is not only needed but actively to be pursued: in addiction treatments, anger management programmes, enforced dieting for the obese, punitive exercise regimes; all of these have arisen, not co-incidentally, in a period of financial 'boom and bust' from which the European world, in particular, has already suffered sickening blows of nemesis. The question is: can these

---

important than 'power' in the riddle of the meaning of desire.

30. It is of course ironic that Foucault himself, in his later writings, gave so much attention to Cassian in expanding his theory of sexuality, power and the 'laboratory of the self'; his insights are in many respects profound, but they cannot help with the final *theological* questions that Cassian himself raises. See Michel Foucault, ed. Jeremy R. Carette, *Religion and Culture* (New York: Routledge, 1999), ch. 15; and Foucault, ed. Michel Senallart, *On the Government of the Living* (Basingstoke: Palgrave/ Macmillian, 2014), chs 11, 12, for comments on Cassian.

secular 'ascetic' treatments themselves succeed without true sociality-in-God?[31]

Conclusions: Returning to God –
The Ecclesiastical Sex Crises and Beyond

The churches, it must be said, have manifestly not been doing well in this climate of complex cultural paradoxicality on the body. Indeed, as I suggested at the start of this Introduction, they have become the veritable lightning rods for the cultural failures, duplicities and anxieties associated with it. Moreover, to suggest that 'asceticism' is the answer to the sexual abuses, homophobia and patriarchal dominance that many still see as endemic to post-World-War-II Roman Catholicism will meet with hollow incredulity unless we first identify the forms of authoritarianism that sustained both that (earlier, counterfeit) asceticism that reigned before Vatican II and its accompanying aberrations.[32] In short, re-summoning 'God', as mere rhetoric, is no quick fix to a deeply complex situation in which so much

---

31. The 'Twelve-Step Programme' of Alcoholics Anonymous famously insists that nothing will work for addiction without the mutual support of a group and the appeal to a 'higher power'.

32. In the popular realm, such authoritarian religious asceticism-gone-wrong is unforgettably summoned in the autobiographical writings of Karen Armstrong (*The Spiral Staircase* [New York: Alfred A. Knopf, 2004]) and John Cornwell (*Seminary Boy: A Memoir* [New York: Doubleday, 2006]). My point here is that such accounts should be read discerningly as cautionary tales, not as revelations of the fruitlessness and corruptibility of asceticism, *tout court*.

ill has been done in the Name.[33] A deeper analysis is needed. In Anglicanism the picture is of course different from that of Roman Catholicism, but no less spiritually tangled and morally fraught: divisive debates over women's ordination to the priesthood and episcopacy have been weirdly trumped of late by the more emotive subject of homosexuality and demands for gay marriage.[34] Thus, whereas the Anglican communion is clearly currently in a different 'place' in debates about gender and sex than the Roman Catholic church at large and the *Magisterium* in particular,[35] it is the project

33. It should be stressed that neither 'asceticism' nor 'prayer' can be used as *enforced* solutions to the riddle of desire – everything depends on the context, tenor, freedom and fruits of the community in which they are produced and maintained, and the notion of God that inspires and sustains the whole. A more profound argument thus has to be mounted that the trinitarian God, properly understood, holds the key to resistance to abuse and transformation into Love: see ch. 3, *intra,* for a further development of this theme.

34. The best sustained *theological* discussion of these debates so far available is to be found in the special issue of the *Anglican Theological Review* 93 (2011), where conservative and liberal voices are both well represented. This discussion was commissioned by the Bishops of the Episcopal Church in America.

35. An insightful and succinct account of current official Roman Catholic teaching on the body, sexuality, and gender is provided by Linda Hogan in her article 'Conflicts within the Roman Catholic Church', in ed. Adrian Thatcher, *The Oxford Handbook of Theology, Sexuality and Gender* (Oxford: Oxford University Press, 2015), pp. 323–39; not insignificantly, she ends her survey with the remark, 'There is a large and growing chasm between the Roman Catholic Church's approach to sex and gender and the views and practices of a significant number of Catholics worldwide' (ibid, p. 336). It is also clear that the Anglican/Roman Catholic line on many of the issues discussed in this book is muddied

of this book to begin to divulge the deeper cultural and theological *aporiai* which these churches share, and which demand the acutest theological attention if any long-term resolution is to be found.

What then *is* 'desire', this book asks, as a constellating category in relation to the divine and to human life? And how do we rightly modulate and direct it, if not by an 'asceticism' that itself yields to that subtle but ecstatic plenitude of divine desire freely outpoured in the life of Christ, and whose test and measure is an extension of that transforming

---

and difficult to traverse with ease: the two churches' abuse scandals, for instance (see ch. 1, *intra*), have tended to take rather different forms, especially where Roman Catholic *religious* life is concerned – that religious life has for so long been backed and protected by central ecclesial authority, whereas Anglican religious life has tended to be 'alternative', for a long time a 'safe' place to be (celibate) gay, though perhaps no longer. On the other hand, while the Catholic *Magisterium* has produced major encyclicals on reproduction, marriage, the body and gender, and love and desire, Anglicanism has clearly gone much further down the road in actual theological discussion of homosexual marriage and of women's priestly ministry. The aversion in official Roman Catholicism even to discussing the 'erotic' disturbance that is to be caused by allowing a woman at the altar, or homosexual men in marriage, is something that bespeaks a true sense that these developments 'change the body' (ecclesial, political), as the Catholic anthropologist Mary Douglas was so right to underscore (see ch. 2, *intra*); and by the same token, as this book repeatedly urges, all questions of individual ascetic demand have immediate implications for wider communities. Much then will depend here ultimately on what underlying theory of 'natural law' holds; and this is where – as I argue finally in ch. 5 – the Anglican tradition reaching back to the early-modern thinker Richard Hooker may have something important to offer in connection with the current debates on sexuality, since Hooker subscribed not to Thomist natural law but to a dynamic alternative allowing for ongoing change.

love to the world? It is to these theologically demanding but existentially urgent questions that I return again and again in the little essays that follow.

I

ECCLESIASTICAL SEX SCANDALS: THE LACK OF A CONTEMPORARY THEOLOGY OF DESIRE

Introduction: The Training of Desire

IN THE LATE FOURTH CENTURY GREGORY OF NYSSA, THE younger brother of Basil of Caesarea and one of the great Cappadocian Fathers who forged the 'orthodox' doctrine of the Trinity in response to late Arianism, wrote a remarkable treatise 'On Virginity' which has puzzled his readership ever since.[1] The reason for this puzzlement – which has, if anything, intensified of late, leading to a string of competing interpretative articles about what Gregory could possibly have meant in this treatise – lies in the fact that Gregory was almost certainly married at the time of his writing of it. Is his high praise of virginity – a life-style embraced by his admired elder brother, Basil – therefore merely *rhetorical*,

---

1. Gregory of Nyssa, 'On Virginity', trans. William Moore, in *Nicene and Post-Nicene Fathers of the Christian Church*, Second Series, vol. 5 (Peabody, MA: Hendrickson, 1995), pp. 343–71. For commentary, see especially Mark D. Hart, 'Gregory of Nyssa's Ironic Praise of the Celibate Life', *The Heythrop Journal* 33 (1992), 1–19; idem, 'Reconciliation of Body and Soul: Gregory of Nyssa's Deeper Theology of Marriage', *Theological Studies* 51 (1990), 450–78; and Valerie A. Karras, 'A Re-evaluation of Marriage, Celibacy, and Irony in Gregory of Nyssa's *On Virginity*', *Journal of Early Christian Studies* 13 (2005), 111–21.

even 'ironic'? Or does his insight about the particular values of married life, too, succumb to an inflated rhetoric: does marriage simply pale, finally, alongside what he perceives as the infinitely higher vocation of celibacy? Or is it neither of these messages, exactly, that he propounds, but something more subtle? I think the latter, as I shall be arguing in due course. For what Gregory presents to us, in this unique text, is a vision of desire – and its right ordering in relation to God – that (puzzlingly to the modern mind, as indeed for the most part to the ancient) does *not* require a disjunctive approach to marriage and celibacy. Rather, it entertains the thought that the godly ordering of desire is what *conjoins* the ascetic aims of marriage and celibacy, at their best, and equally what judges both of them, at their worst. Thus, at the height of his argument in the *de virginitate* Gregory can write that the choice for his reader is whether ultimately to be a 'Pleasure-lover' or a 'God-lover', that is, to make a choice about what the *final* telos of one's desire is. Not that sexual pleasure holds any intrinsic fear for him, unlike for his near contemporary in the West, Augustine of Hippo, whose epic and tortured struggles for sexual continence we know about in detail from the *Confessions*.[2] Rather, says Gregory, it is all a matter of due balance or 'proportion'. The key issue, in fact, for Gregory, is a *training* of desire, a life-long commitment to what we might now call the 'long haul' of personal, erotic transformation, and thereby of reflection on the final significance of all one's desires before God.

---

2. Augustine, *Confessions*, trans. Henry Chadwick (Oxford: Oxford University Press, 1998).

Such a reference as this to an obscure, and puzzling, text of the patristic era might seem an odd place to open a discussion of the contemporary sex crises of the Roman Catholic and Anglican churches. But there is a method in my madness. For I seek, in this chapter, to outline, first, some of the problematic features of the journalistic – or 'high popular' – responses to the sex crises in both the Catholic and Anglican churches, and to indicate how strangely lacking here is a distinctively *theological* analysis of the fundamental issue of desire. Several well-publicized journalist volumes on the crises have appeared and are of varying quality and insight: they range from Steinfels's highly nuanced historical assessment of the Roman Church's current crises, through Sipe's largely psychological account of celibacy, via Greeley's sociological riposte to Sipe's pessimism on the priesthood, to the troublingly voyeuristic journalism of sexual abuse in France's account, as also in Berry and Renner.[3] But my initial point here is that historical, political, sociological, and above all psychological theories abound about the causes for the scandals in the Roman Catholic Church, as indeed also for the threatened schism in the Anglican Communion.[4] Yet

---

3. Peter Steinfels, *A People Adrift: The Crisis of the Roman Catholic Church in America* (New York: Simon and Schuster, 2003); A. W. Richard Sipe, *Celibacy in Crisis: A Secret World Revisited* (New York: Brunner-Routledge, 2003); Andrew M. Greeley, *Priests: A Calling in Crisis* (Chicago, IL: University of Chicago Press, 2004); David France, *Our Fathers: The Secret Life of the Catholic Church in an Age of Scandal* (New York: Broadway, 2004); Jason Berry and Gerald Renner, *Vows of Silence: The Abuse of Power in the Papacy of John Paul II* (New York: Free Press, 2004).

4. On the latter, see Stephen Bates, *A Church at War: Anglicans and*

there is very little that could be called a sustained *theological* analysis of the problem of human sexual desire encoded in these two notable ecclesial furores.

However, some striking 'cultural contradictions'[5] underlie these journalistic responses. Despite their own suppression of the theological, such responses are potentially more teasing and suggestive than the 'official', disjunctive theological opinions ('conservative' vs. 'liberal') that are currently overlaid like a clamping template upon them. 'Conservatives' here, of course, tend to have recourse either to biblical injunctions, which they take to be unambiguous, or to magisterial authority, often expressed, understandably, with a high degree of suspicion for modern, secular post-Freudian reflections on sexuality. 'Liberals', in contrast, tend to suggest, overbearingly, that they know better (in the light of modern psychological theory) than anything that the Bible or tradition or authority could disclose to them. The battle lines are then inexorably fixed. And it is of course this disjunction between religious 'conservatives' and 'liberals' that tends to dominate the headlines, and further stultify any newly *creative* theological way forward as the two parties retire into their entrenched bunkers of mutual hostility and suspicion.

The central thesis of this chapter, then, is that there is another mode of discussion that could cut creatively across the established ecclesial battle-lines — 'liberal' and 'conservative',

---

Homosexuality (London: Tauris, 2004).

5. For this term, see Daniel Bell, *The Cultural Contradictions of Capitalism* (New York: Basic Books, 2nd edn, 1996).

'pro-gay' and 'anti-gay' – and draw both camps into a new, and serious, reflection on *ascetical theology*, *tout court*. It is true that in order to get to where I want to be I am deliberately avoiding the usual pitfalls of a discussion that starts with, and then gets bogged down in, contentious biblical passages on 'sodomy': in short, I am not beginning with what might be called a 'biblical/ethical' approach. Instead I want first to establish, and negotiate, a new interaction between Freud, on the one hand, and pre-modern ascetical theologies such as Gregory's, on the other, which the journalistic mind may indeed find fantastic, but which could be much more rich and strange than is expected. This will not, note, be a feeble kind of *via media*, the sort of compromised *rapprochement* between a secular ideology and a religious tradition that a study of the origins of the Anglican Communion might lead one to expect of me, an Anglican theologian. No, it will actually be an exposure of the richness, complexity and *unfinished* nature of Freud's notion of 'sublimation', such that we are forced back to its sources in Plato and his Christian inheritors, and required to think afresh on matters that Freud himself never definitively parsed. Such, then, is the modest task of this brief undertaking. I cannot, of course, *solve* our current cultural dilemmas on the inexorable nature of human desire; but I do at least hope to muse creatively in such a way that new paths of theological discussion can be opened up.

The Sex Scandals and 'Cultural Contradictions'

Anyone who has attentively followed the press coverage of

the recent sex scandals in the Roman Catholic Church, on the one hand, and of the ecclesiastical divisions over homosexuality in the Anglican Communion, on the other, may have become aware of certain pressing contemporary 'cultural contradictions' on matters of sexuality and desire that these two crises enshrine, and to which I now wish to draw explicit attention. It might be objected that even to name these two areas of ecclesial public furore thus in one breath is already to have committed a dire, and offensive, fallacy of 'castigation by lumping'[6]; for surely the abusive and illegal activities of paedophile Roman Catholic priests must *in no wise* be conflated with the honest and open vowed relationships of gay Episcopalians, including one of such who is now a bishop? To this we must reply immediately that *of course* the difference is ethically crucial – not only in the eyes of the law, but in terms of the unequal power relationships, and the protective shroud of ecclesiastical secrecy, that have marked the Roman Catholic scandal in contrast to the Anglican scandal. Yet at the same time one cannot help noticing, simply by reflecting on the odd temporal coincidence of these two, very different, ecclesiastical paroxysms over same-sex desire, that a latent 'cultural contradiction' of great significance is here made manifest. There is a deep and pervasive public pessimism, on the one hand, over the very *possibility* of faithful celibacy, and yet an equally deep insistence that *certain* forms of sexual desire must at all costs not be enacted.

---

6. To use one of Jeffrey Stout's memorable phrases. See, e.g., his *Democracy and Tradition* (Princeton, NJ: Princeton University Press, 2004), p. 128.

This first cultural contradiction was forcefully, if perhaps unconsciously, expressed by Garry Wills in his famous article 'The Case Against Celibacy'. Wills writes: 'The whole celibacy structure is a house of cards, and honesty about any one problem can make the structure of pretense come toppling down ... Treating paedophilia as a separate problem is impossible, since it thrives by its place in a compromised network of evasion ... [The] real enemy is celibacy.'[7] Yet at the beginning of the same article Wills had inveighed against 'the worst aspect' of the crisis, 'the victimization of the young' and 'the clerical epidemic of ... crimes'.[8] In other words, celibacy is impossible, compromising and delusive. The whole system smacks of unreality; yet those who do have unmanageable and illegal desires must be held to account and punished: they must and *should* be celibate. Herein, then, we detect our first, and profound, 'cultural contradiction': celibacy is impossible, but celibacy *must* be embraced by some with unacceptable and illegal desires.

Now of course once the familiar 'liberal'/'conservative' divide is imposed on this first 'cultural contradiction', we get a certain diversion from it and an ostensibly much clearer disjunction: the 'liberals' happily condone faithful vowed gay relationships but condemn illegal and abusive paedophile ones, and the 'conservatives' – whether Protestant or Catholic – disavow and ban all of them by appeal to biblical injunctions against sodomy, or with reference to 'natural'

---

7. Garry Wills, 'The Case Against Celibacy', *The Boston Globe Magazine*, 24 March 2002, 10–24 (22, 24).

8. Wills, 'Case', 10.

law. *This* division (between 'pro-gay' and 'anti-gay', 'liberals' and 'conservatives'), however, then tends to get most of the public attention in ecclesiastical circles and in the press, thus diverting us from the underlying and unsolved cultural conundrum: how can sexual control be demanded of *anyone* if celibacy is intrinsically 'impossible'? To this issue we shall shortly return.

A second 'cultural contradiction' seems to afflict the treatment of homosexual desire versus heterosexual desire in contemporary popular discussion of church divisions. For it has been a marked feature of both the Roman Catholic and Anglican sex-crises that almost all the press attention has been focused on same-sex relationships, whether paedophile, 'ephebophile', or (mature) homosexual. It is as if, by comparison, no crisis at all has afflicted the *heterosexual* world *vis-à-vis* church life and what we might call the general 'economy of desire'. But anyone surveying the cultural and political scene with a dispassionate eye would surely be forced to come to other conclusions. The general erosion of the instance of life-long marriage in North America, the rise in divorce rates, and the concomitant upsurge in the number of single-parent families, are all well known to us in secular discussions, but are by no means absent from church-attending families, and indeed Protestant *clerical* families. In April 2005, for instance, the clergy of an Episcopalian Diocese in New England received a mailing calmly announcing that one of their suffragan bishops was undergoing a divorce. One could not but be struck by the air of enforced 'normalcy' and psychological adjudication that hung over this letter. There were no regrets, no confessions, no distress even, and certainly no reference to either biblical or Christian tradition: just an insistence that the couple had been 'faithful in caring for ... each other' in the past, but were now 'clear' about the fact that their marriage was 'ending'. Clergy were further informed by their suffragan bishop, in psychologized language: 'I want to assure you that I am taking *care of myself* in this *period of change*.' Apart from one reference to an 'excellent Spiritual Director' that the bishop had now decided to see, there was no theological reference in her letter at all. I wish to cast no specific judgments on this case since I have no independent information about it at all, and even if I had, the matter would surely be morally complex and demand due compassion. But in fact, the news of the ending of this marriage makes me much sadder than the letter would seem to warrant. I cite the case only to note an instance of the current culturally condoned acknowledgement of the impermanence of marriage, even in the ranks of bishops.

Yet my more important, second point here is this: despite the extensive evidences of clerical divorce, and (quite differently) of clerical abuse or philandering, both Catholic and Protestant, in *heterosexual* encounters or relationships, the more emotive issue of clerical *homoerotic* desire currently tends to continue to glean much greater public attention in the press and related publications than anything to do with heterosexual sex. It is as if, suddenly in early twenty-first century America, homoeroticism has become sufficiently open to discussion to be publicly, and emotively, dissected in the press, and then either condoned or condemned. It is, however, insufficiently integrated into a *general* discussion of 'desire' to make comparisons with heterosexual patterns of behaviour a worthy topic of sustained theological reflection. Yet one might well say that our age is in a crisis – not so much of homosexuality, but more generally of erotic *faithfulness*.[9] However, this is scarcely a chic reflection, granted the current prurient obsession with homosexuality, and the concomitant diversion from heterosexual failures in ascetic self-examination.

A third and final 'cultural contradiction' that I want to propose hovers over the common assumption that celibacy and marriage are somehow *opposites*, with one ostensibly involving no 'sex' at all, and the other, again supposedly, involving as much sex as one or both partners might like at any one time. But this, on reflection, is also a perplexing cultural fantasy that does not bear close, analytic scrutiny. The 'ethnographic' evidence provided in Richard Sipe's book *Celibacy in Crisis* is revealing here. Not only does faithful (or what Sipe calls 'achieved') celibacy generally involve, perforce, a *greater* consciousness of sexual desire and its frustration than a life lived with regular sexual satisfaction (that attacks one side of the false presumption);[10] but married sexuality, on the other hand, is rarely as carefree and mutually satisfied as this third 'cultural contradiction' might presume. Indeed, a *realistic* reflection on long and faithful marriages

---

9. On this same point see David Brooks, 'The Power of Marriage', The *New York Times,* 22 November 2003, A15.

10. See Sipe, *Celibacy*, especially chs 3, 12, 13.

(now almost in the minority) will surely reveal periods of enforced 'celibacy' even *within* marriages during periods of delicate pregnancy, parturition, illness, physical separation, or impotence, which are simply the lot of the marital 'long haul', realistically considered. And if this is so, then the generally assumed disjunction between 'celibacy' and 'marriage' will turn out to be not as profound as it seems. Rather, the reflective, faithful celibate and the reflective, faithful married person may have more in common – by way of prayerful surrendering of inevitably *thwarted* desire to God – than the unreflective or faithless celibate, or the carelessly happy, or indeed unhappily careless, married person.

We shall return fleetingly to these three 'cultural contradictions' I have outlined at the end of this chapter. We cannot go further now, however, without attacking a different sort of cultural presumption head-on: that of the supposed psychological *dangers* of celibacy or of so-called 'repressed' sexuality. But we may here be surprised to discover what Freud himself said on this matter, and to him we shall now turn. Could it be that he actually gives us, despite himself, certain back-handed resources for thinking afresh *theologically* about 'desire'?

The Re-channelling of Desire: Freud and His Precursors
1. Freud on 'Sublimation': Desire Without God

The journalistic commentators on the Roman Catholic sex crises tend to take the view, as we have mentioned, that celibacy is 'impossible', or virtually so. Even Sipe – who wishes, despite his sustained exposé of clerical failures in celibacy, to defend the estimated 2% of Roman Catholic priests who he thinks (as he puts it) 'achieve' celibacy – avers that this 'achievement' is always at the cost of earlier 'experimentation' and fumbling, through which the priest must inevitably pass *en route* to something like mature sexual balance.[11] These analyses are gloomy: Sipe estimates that nearly half of so-called 'celibates' are actually not so at any one time. Underlying these accounts seems to lurk the psychological presumption, often attributed to Freud, that celibacy is unnatural and even harmful; or if not *inherently* 'unnatural', then distinctly 'unusual' and 'utopian'.[12] It might come as some surprise, then, to find that Freud's own views on 'sublimation' were not only malleable over time, remaining finally somewhat unclear and inconsistent, but that he moved distinctly away from his early, and purely biological, account of 'Eros' and its power for redirection. At no time, in fact (as far as I can see), does Freud's position provide a mandate for the view that 'sublimation' is *harmful* – or, at any rate, any more harmful than the psychological repressions we necessarily negotiate all the time, according to Freud. On the contrary, as I shall now sketch, Freud's later view is that if civilization is to endure we must all be engaged in forms of 'sublimation', and that celibacy has always been the choice of a 'minority' who interpret this pressure 'religiously'.

Two points about Freud on sexual desire seem particu-

---

11. Sipe, *Celibacy*, pp. 301–2.

12. For such a minority report amongst journalistic commentators, see Steinfels, *A People Adrift*, p. 330. Steinfels is considerably more charitable than most American journalists on celibacy.

larly intriguing in our quest for a revitalized *theological* account of such desire. The first is that we can trace a distinct change in his views on 'Eros' from his early writings on the biological drive of sex in *The Interpretation of Dreams* and the *Lectures on Psychoanalysis*, through a transitional period represented by *Beyond the Pleasure Principle*, to a mature sensibility about the possible re-channelling of 'erotic' power in a less biological and less repressive sense, in *Civilization and Its Discontents* and *Why War?*[13] These shifts are highly illuminating and show how unafraid Freud was to change his mind, indeed, how his mind — even when changed — remained somewhat unclear on the matter as late as the 1930s. The shifts particularly give the lie to the popular misconstrual that Freud sees sublimation/repression as inevitably *harmful*. In his early writings, Freud rarely uses the word 'Eros', although when he does it is as a synonym for the 'Libido', the physical, biological, sexual drive which at this stage, he argues, often comes into conflict with the 'Ego'. Note that, even in this early phase, Freud is by no means of the opinion that it is harmful to *resist* physical sexual expression in all circumstances. He stresses, for instance, how harmful

---

13. Sigmund Freud, *The Interpretation of Dreams*, ed. Ritchie Robertson, trans. Joyce Crick (Oxford: Oxford University Press, 1999 [1900]); idem, *New Introductory Lectures on Psychoanalysis*, trans. James Strachey (New York: Norton, 1985 [1916–17]); idem, *Beyond the Pleasure Principle*, trans. Strachey (New York: Norton, 1975 [1920]); idem, *Civilization and Its Discontents*, trans. Strachey (New York: Norton, 1989 [1929–30]); idem, 'Why War?' [an open letter to Albert Einstein], in *Civilization, War and Death: Selections from Three Works by Sigmund Freud*, ed. John Rickman (London: Hogarth, 1939 [1933]), pp. 82–97.

sexual activity itself can often be, precisely because its significance is social and not merely individual. 'Sexuality', he
writes, has 'advantages, but, in return for an unusually high
degree of pleasure, brings dangers which threaten the individual's life and often destroy it.'[14] Eros at this stage, then,
is conceived biologically, and as always in a state of restless
negotiation and tension: it must *necessarily* be repressed in
part, and hence its difficulties.

By 1920, however, Freud significantly extends his concept of Libido and more consistently labels it 'Eros'. He also
draws the Ego and the Libido closer together, rather than
placing them in conflict; Eros/Libido have come now to
include not just *biological* sex drive but all of the Ego's instincts to self-preservation and the maintenance of life. At
this point, too, Freud first introduces the notion of Thanatos
(death) as a new binary opposite to Eros: whereas Eros is
the drive that presses towards the future and new life, Thanatos looks backwards and is death-obsessed. In short, Freud
has created a new binary, more publicly oriented than the
earlier individual psychic tension between Ego and Libido,
and which provides a sort of Hegelian dialectic of *cultural*
propulsion. No wonder, then, that his later theory of 'sublimation' (*Aufhebung* in German) has a wider cultural remit
than his earlier account of individual biological needs and
their necessary repressions. This new theory – expressed in
Civilization and its Discontents and then, slightly differently,
in *Why War?* – is now fascinatingly, and explicitly, linked to
Plato's theory of erotic 'ascent' to Beauty in the *Symposium*,

14. Freud, *New Introductory Lectures*, p. 413.

and it is 'what makes it possible for higher psychical activities, whether scientific, artistic or ideological, to play such an important part in civilized life'.[15] Although in *Civilization*, Freud remains of the opinion that such culturally conceived *Aufhebung* comes with the danger and cost of a necessary accompanying 'renunciation' or 'repression',[16] it is far from clear that he consistently maintains this position later. As Marcuse argued, there seems to be in Freud yet another strand on 'sublimation' that does *not* involve repression, but rather a more straightforward transference of aggressive energy to a good, 'erotic' end.[17] Thus, in the course of a striking correspondence of 1933 initiated by Albert Einstein, Freud can express the astonishingly optimistic view, as war-clouds gathered in Europe, that 'Erotism' – the love instinct – could finally triumph over Hate and war and aggression (Thanatos), by a sort of *direct* transference of the energies of hate. As he now puts it to Einstein, love and hate must always go together, so that one – love – can modify or redirect the energies of the other – hate. '*Complete* suppression of man's aggressive tendencies', he concludes, 'is not in issue; what we try is to *divert it into a channel* other than that

---

15. E.g., Freud, *Why War?*, p. 90; quotation from idem, *Civilization*, p. 51. See Plato, *The Symposium*, trans. Walter Hamilton (London: Penguin, 1951).

16. Freud, *Civilization*, p. 52.

17. Herbert Marcuse, 'The transformation of sexuality into eros', in *Eros and Civilization: A Philosophical Inquiry into Freud* (Boston: Beacon, 1974), pp. 197–221.

of warfare.'[18] Note, then, that a discussion of 'sublimation', which started in Freud's early works as a matter related to mere biological drive, has now become a theory of a *positive*, and seemingly non-repressive, 're-channelling' of psychic energy. Let us keep this theme of positive 're-channelling' in mind when we go back to Christian authors later: we might find more continuity with Freud, via the shared resource of Plato, than we may expect.

The second point about Freud on 'sublimation' that I want to stress here, however, is the issue on which he is most at odds with Christianity, and indeed with Plato. And this too is instructive, at least backhandedly, for our theological purposes, and again, not what one might expect to hear from him. For when Freud speaks about specifically *Christian* celibacy he does not inveigh against it, nor deride it as psychically dangerous or impossible – though he does say that it is only a 'small minority' who are 'enabled by their constitution to find happiness, in spite of everything' according to this path. Rather, he says – *à la* Plato's first stages of erotic ascent in the *Symposium* – that celibates have managed to direct their love to 'all men alike' rather than simply to *one*, chosen sexual 'love-object'.[19] It is precisely 'religion' that helps them to do this, he admits; and, as we might expect from Freud, this causes him to inject a sneer. It is not that he thinks celibacy is intrinsically damaging, but rather that he has *moral* objections to the 'religious' idea that one should love everyone equally. First he writes: 'A love

18. Freud in Einstein and Freud, 'Why War?', pp. 91, 93, my emphasis.

19. See Freud, *Civilization*, pp. 56–8.

that does not discriminate seems to me to forfeit a part of its own value.' He goes on: 'not all men are *worthy* of love'.[20] What this rhetoric hides, it seems to me, is a deep abiding *aporia* in Freud's new, but partial, accommodation of Plato. Since there is no final theory of 'forms' for Freud, still less a Christian God, then the newly embraced Platonic ladder of ascent leads nowhere: 'Eros' lacks eschatological, or *divine,* direction. Thus, while celibacy remains both possible, and even undamaging, for the later Freud, he cannot accept its *moral* goals, and nor can he give it final *theological* meaning.

2. Anders Nygren as Distractor: *Eros* and *Agape* disjoined

If we have now successfully shown, then, that Freud himself – as opposed to the contemporary popular American mis-understanding of him – sees 'sublimation' as personally and culturally *necessary*, and even priestly celibacy as *possible*, wherein lies the continuing felt resistance to a contempo-rary *theology* of desire? We have seen how Freud, motivated by sheer atheistical conviction, himself blocks the upward ascent of 'Eros' towards any heavenly goal. It might, howev-er, be that Anders Nygren's famous study *Agape and Eros* (which originally appeared in Swedish in 1930-6), rather than the secular Freud, has actually played a wider cultural role here than is normally recognized in undermining a modern Christian theology of 'desire'. A twentieth-century classic, the book's rigidly Lutheran (and oft-criticized) the-sis is so well known as scarcely to need another rehearsal. *Agape*, claims Nygren, is the Christian love of Jesus in the

---

20. Freud, *Civilization*, p. 57, my emphasis.

New Testament – graced, God-given, sacrificial, down-ward-moving, unselfish; whereas nasty Platonic *eros* or 'desire' is, in contrast, acquisitive, man-centred, upward-moving, egocentric, and needy. To again pick up our metaphor of 'channelling', we may note how frightened Nygren is about the possibility of *any* safe channelling of the alarming erotic urge: 'The idea of Agape', he writes, 'can be compared to a *small stream* which, even in the history of Christianity, flows along an extremely narrow channel and sometimes seems to lose itself entirely in its surrounding; but Eros is a *broad river that overflows its banks*, carrying everything away with it, so that it is not easy even in thought to dam it up and make it flow in an orderly course'.[21] I mention Nygren's thesis here only briefly as a bridge back to our discussion of Gregory of Nyssa and other pre-modern Christian theorizers of 'desire'. This is because anyone who wishes, as I now do, to re-engage a significant dimension of Christian tradition that consciously married the New Testament with Platonic and neo-Platonic ideas of *eros*, inevitably has to run Nygren's gauntlet. It is worth pointing out, then, with earlier critics of Nygren, that while his account of New Testament views of *agape* is relatively accurate, his reading of Platonic *eros* is by contrast highly selective, negative and contentious.[22] It shows little cognizance even of the subtlety of Diotima's speech on the nature of love in Plato's *Symposium*,

21. Anders Nygren, *Agape and Eros*, trans. Philip S. Watson (London: SPCK, 1953), pp. 49–50, my emphasis.

22. Especially Martin C. D'Arcy, *The Mind and Heart of Love* (London: Faber, 1954).

in which the ladder of erotic purification is mounted in order finally to '*have* disclosed' to her 'suddenly' – and as a sort
of gift or revelation – a *participation* in the form of Beauty.
This is no mere selfish 'grasping'. Not only is Nygren's
reading of Plato marred by an imposition of Christian, and
specifically Lutheran, fears of 'works righteousness' and of
Pelagianism. It also has the effect of placing sexual attrac-
tion and '*Christian* love' in radically different boxes with no
obvious means of mutual influence – a Protestant trait,
which has lethal consequences for any theological theorizing
of sexuality and its relation to God's love. To move towards
our own constructive proposal, based on Gregory of Nyssa's
seminal insights, we shall have simply to bypass Nygren's
roadblock and declare it a mistaken and false construction.
Nygren is in fact quite unable, on account of his rigid binary,
to give any positive account of the alliance of Christian *agape*
and Platonic *eros* that began in the third century with Hippolytus and Origen and their commentaries on the Song of
Songs, and passed from them to Nyssen; and yet this was the
marriage that was to spawn innumerable classics of 'mystical
theology' thereafter. For Origen, *agape* simply *is eros*, by any
other name; whereas for his rather different successor in the
Song-commentary tradition, Gregory of Nyssa, *eros* is *agape*
(as he puts it) 'stretched out in longing' towards the divine
goal. Let us therefore turn back, in the final section of this
chapter, to see further how Nyssen's views on celibacy curiously *cohere* with his views on marriage, and how his insights

might steer us beyond the false 'cultural contradictions' with which we started this chapter.

3. Platonic *eros* and Christian appropriation: Gregory of Nyssa

We have been charting, in the cases of both Freud and Nygren, how the image of 'channelling' is used in relation to erotic desire in interestingly contrastive ways. For Freud, it provides a means of positive transference of energies, whereas for Nygren the dangerous 'eros' is forever destructively bursting its banks. Precisely this same image of channelling, interestingly, is at the heart of Gregory of Nyssa's theorizing of marriage and celibacy in his *de virginitate*. As Valerie Karras perceptively shows in her excellent article on this treatise, Gregory is being 'ironic', neither in his adulation of celibacy nor of marriage, puzzling as it may seem that they should be put thus together.[23] The really interesting and unique heart of the argument, then, lies in the metaphor of the 'stream' of desire, and of its right direction, use, and even *intensification* in relation to God. As far as Gregory is concerned, celibates and married people are equally involved in this task as a life-long ascetical exercise. He writes:

> Imagine a stream flowing from a spring and dividing itself off into a number of accidental channels. As long as it proceeds so, it will be useless for any purpose of agriculture, the dissipation of its waters making each particular current small and feeble, and therefore slow. But if one were to mass these wandering and widely dispersed rivulets again

---

23. See Karras, 'Re-evaluation', *passim.*

into one single channel, he would have a full and collected stream for the supplies which life demands. Just so the
human mind ... as long as its current spreads itself in all
directions over the pleasures of the senses, has no power
that is worth the naming of making its way towards the
Real Good; but once call it back and collect it upon itself
... it will find no obstacle in mounting to higher things, in
grasping realities.[24]

This compares interestingly with Nygren's imaging of
dangerous and excessive 'erotic' channels. It might be thought
that Gregory intends this intensification of desire towards
God to be mutually exclusive with a sexually active life in
marriage; but interestingly he repeats the same metaphor of
the stream in the following chapter 8, precisely to explain
how sex in marriage can be a 'good irrigation' provided it,
too, is ordered in relation to God and so made 'moderate'
in comparison with the intensified and unified stream that
desire for God demands. The treatise is not written, then,
to *suppress* 'passion'; but actually (as stated by Gregory at the
very outset) precisely to '*create passion*' for 'the life according to excellence'. Married sexual expression, and its erotic
metaphors, thus hold no worries for Gregory – unlike for
Augustine, who was to find even lawful married intercourse
a matter for concern on account of its capacity for male loss
of 'control'[25], and who notably never expanded any theology of the Song of Songs as did Gregory later. Here, in the

---

24. Gregory, 'On Virginity' 7, p. 352.

25. Augustine, *The City of God Against the Pagans* 14.16, trans. R. W. Dy-
son (Cambridge: Cambridge University Press, 1998), pp. 614–15.

earlier *de virginitate*, however, Gregory lauds 'virginity' *not* on account of its sexlessness, but because of its withdrawal from *worldly* interests – the building up of families, status and honour – and hence its emulation of the changeless life of the Trinity. It is not sex that is the problem, but worldly values. And he sees a good, spiritually productive marriage as almost on a par with celibacy given its equal potential capacity, when desire is rightly 'aimed', to bear the fruits of *leitourgia*, 'service' to others, especially to the poor. Consequently, by the end of the treatise, as Valerie Karras rightly shows, we have an instructive set of hierarchically ordered possibilities for 'erotic' states of affairs: bad marriage, in which the external rules of fidelity may be kept but no spiritual unification of desire towards God occurs – no right 'channelling' of *eros*; bad celibacy, in which the external rules likewise may, or may not, be obeyed, but in which physical virginity is not leading to any transformation of the soul; and then spiritually fruitful marriage and spiritually fruitful celibacy, which in contrast both turn out to have more in common with one another than do the other states. Hence, as Karras puts it, the married person who can 'channel the water' erotically towards God is significantly above the mere *physically* celibate virgin who is still subject to false attachments or the 'spiritual' vices of envy, malice and slander.[26] But the special power of the virgin who has also rightly channelled the erotic stream lies, for Gregory, in his significance for others. Gregory ends, much in the spirit of Alasdair MacIntyre to-

---

26. Karras, 'Re-evaluation', p. 121.

day,[27] with an insistence that ascetical *practices* are means of transformation and of the indispensable spiritual power of a person from whom one may *mimetically* 'catch the halo', as he puts it, of rightly ordered desire. In other words – and this is surely a point of great spiritual significance today – rightly channelled *eros*, whether married or celibate, is impossible without deep prayer and ascetic perseverance; but it is even more impossible, interestingly, without shining examples to emulate. Such, for Gregory himself, was the inspiration of his celibate brother Basil: celibacy was ultimately to be 'caught', not 'taught'.

Conclusions: Beyond Repression and Libertinism

Let me now gather the strands of this chapter. As we have seen, Nyssen's tract 'On Virginity' is unique and puzzling in the tradition precisely because it is written by a married person and cuts across the usual dividing categories of lay and ordained, married and celibate. As such, I suggest, it not only provides a potential hermeneutical key for reading other forms of ascetic literature against the grain and across traditional disjunctions (so that literature for monastics can be given lay application), but surely also gives the lie to Peter Steinfels's insistence that a celibate clergy could only now be re-invigorated within contemporary Roman Catholicism *at the cost of* a continuing high theology of lay and married service. As Steinfels puts it: 'If the church wants to restore celi-

27. See Alasdair MacIntyre, *After Virtue: A Study in Moral Theory* (London: Duckworth, 3rd edn, 2007), for his re-enunciated emphasis on the importance of 'practice' in the moral life.

bacy to [its] former status, there is really only one practical way to do it: demote marriage to the second-class standing it once had."[28] It has been the burden of this chapter to suggest otherwise, in the spirit of Gregory; and not only to insist that marriage and celibacy should thus be re-thought alongside one another, but also implicitly – and doubtless more contentiously – that heterosexual and homosexual desire should also, and analogously, be reflected on in concert by the same exacting standards of progressive non-attachment and ascetical transformation. Then, I submit, homoerotic desire could potentially be released from its cultural and biblical associations with libertinism, promiscuity and disorder. Gregory's vision of desire as thwarted, chastened, transformed, renewed and finally *intensified* in God, bringing forth spiritual fruits of *agape* and *leitourgia* in a number of different contexts, represents a way beyond and through the false modern alternatives of 'repression' and 'libertinism', between *agape* and *eros*. This way, as I have argued in this chapter, has curiously more points of contact with the real Freud than with the imaginary Freud of American popular consciousness. Whether Gregory's stern intimations of the final locus of desire can also be the means of a sublation of all three of the cultural contradictions I outlined at the start of this chapter I leave to you to decide, but such has been my implicit argument. Certainly the re-thinking of celibacy *and* faithful vowed relations (whether heterosexual or homosexual) in an age of instantly commodified desire and massive infidelity is a task of daunting proportions, in which

28. Steinfels, *A People Adrift*, p. 330.

no-one can be very confident of widespread success. But as Gregory himself warns, we cannot believe it unless we see it lived: 'Any theory divorced from living examples ... is like [an] unbreathing statue.'[29] Therein, perhaps, lies the true challenge for us today: the counter-cultural production, not of film-stars, sports heroes or (sometimes) faithless royal families, but of erotic *saints*.

The conclusion, then, to which I have finally brought us is that we cannot solve our ecclesiastical crises about 'homosexuality' unless we first, all of us, re-imagine theologically the whole project of our human sorting, taming and purifying of desires within the crucible of *divine* desire. Such is the ascetical long haul set before us, in which faithfulness plays the indispensable role endemic to the demands of the primary love for God. To re-think the current ecclesiastical 'homosexuality' crises in *this* light, I have suggested, would be to re-invest the debate with a theological and spiritual wisdom too long forgotten.

---

29. Gregory, 'On Virginity' 23, p. 368.

2

THE WOMAN AT THE ALTAR:
COSMOLOGICAL DISTURBANCE
OR GENDER SUBVERSION?

Introduction: The Priesthood, Gender and Desire

IN THIS CHAPTER, I WISH TO TURN OUR ATTENTION TO the question of how the ascetic life relates to matters of ritual, and specifically to the supreme Christian ritual of the eucharist. More particularly, I want here to develop a speculative line of argument about the nature of Christian priesthood and its connection to eroticism and gender-identification. And I want to do this in a way that embraces, rather than eschews, the traditional symbolism of the eucharist as the enactment of nuptial love between Christ and the Church. This strategy might seem to be a high-risk one for a feminist theologian and woman priest, and indeed it is: it consciously walks right into the fanned flames of passion surrounding the question of female ordination in conservative Roman Catholic and Orthodox circles, where the very idea of women priests is still denounced as intrinsically gender-disordered, indeed as cosmically disturbing to the supposedly 'natural' arrangement of sex-binaries.[1]

---

1. The official Roman Catholic pronouncements against the ordination of women can conveniently be found in The Congregation for the Doctrine of the Faith, *From 'Inter Insigniores' to 'Ordinatio Sacerdotalis'*

A much safer strategy for a feminist theologian, it would seem, would be the *sanitization* of this heady nexus of themes (communion, desire, priestly enactment), by repressing or de-essentializing the symbolism of Christ and his bride, the church. Such a sanitization can be attempted, and of course has been, many times over. The arguments for such sanitization are certainly not without worth, and perhaps should be mentioned here at the start. Three such lines of approach come to mind. One may either, first, on *scriptural or theological grounds*, declare erotic symbolism to be disconnected from the New Testament evidence about the institution of the eucharist as such (as compared with the wider christological symbolism of Eph. 5.21–33), thus only later imposed as a questionable hermeneutical veneer, and now in any case inappropriate to post-Vatican II Catholic ecclesiological sensibilities about the 'pilgrim church'. Or, second, one may urge on *moral grounds* – which today of course are peculiarly pressing – that this nexus fatally confuses the arenas of sexual desire and desire for God in a way inclined subliminally to promote abuse. Or, third, one may insist on an even quicker disposal technique for the nuptial metaphor by taking a stand against it on secular *gender-theoretical grounds*, and seeing it as intrinsically misleading precisely because it is sustaining of repressive and stereotypical 'gender binaries'.

In what follows, however, I shall be exploring none of

(Washington, DC: United States Catholic Conference, 1998). Recent Eastern Orthodox positions are represented in Thomas Hopko, ed., *Women and the Priesthood* (Crestwood, NY: St. Vladimir's Press, revised edn, 1999). Both volumes rehearse and discuss the theme of the presumed 'unnaturalness' of female priesthood.

these well-worn arguments, however important one may judge them to be. Rather, I want to conduct a different sort of thought experiment. I want to see what happens if we relentlessly *pursue* the very logic of the opponents of women priests, that is, if we look more deeply into this problematic nexus of eroticism, gender roles, and priestly mediation of Christ's presence. And (to anticipate my conclusions) I shall be arguing that it is vital so to look – rather than to look *away*; for when we probe the implications of the Christ/church nuptial model more attentively, and reflect on how the priest acts as mediator of that relationship, we shall find it impossible to 'fix' the priest as 'masculine' alone: the conservative argument fails precisely in the complexities of its enactment. On the contrary, I shall argue, the priest is in an inherently fluid gender role as beater of the liminal bounds between the divine and the human. But in representing *both* 'Christ' *and* 'Church' (that is the first rejoinder to the conservatives), the priest is not simply divine/'masculine' in the first over human/'feminine' in the other, but *both* in *both*. Yet this is not, as is sometimes argued, a form of 'androgyny' that either flattens 'difference' or plays down erotic meaning. For in the course of the liturgy the priest moves implicitly through these different roles, strategically summoning the stereotypical gender associations of each, but always destabilizing the attempt to be 'held' in one or the other.[2] In short, the gender binaries that *appear* to be being

---

2. The emphasis on the '*strategic*' summoning of stereotypical binaries here is important, lest I be misheard as simply recommending their continuation. As will emerge as my argument unfolds, I am presuming

re-valorized liturgically (God/active/'masculine', *versus* human/receptive/'feminine') are actually being summoned in order subtly to be undermined.[3]

Finally, if I am right, a significant part of the undeniably 'erotic' tug of the priest's position at the altar lies in this very destabilization, a gesturing towards a divine 'order' of union and communion beyond the tidy human attempts at gender characterization and binary division. Yet the delicacy of such a gesturing cannot simply be predicated on an ideological gender egalitarianism, on the forced *repression* of 'difference'; in this the conservative opponents of women's ordination are right. Where they fail is in the attempt to 'freeze' the gender binaries back into an order that their own very insights betray.

In short, or so it would seem, I shall in this chapter be hoisting the remaining opponents of women's ordination on their own petard. Yet that would actually be a somewhat misleading reading. For I offer these reflections less in the spirit of antagonism than of *rapprochement*: to admit the irreducible significance of the nuptial metaphor is already to

---

that such human binaries do, and will, continue to exercise us in some form, both culturally and theologically; thus 'strategic' attention to them, rather than a forced attempt at their obliteration or repression, is in my view required *en route* to their liturgical transformation. For more on the theme of the transformation of stereotypical binaries, see the last sections of this chapter, below, and notes 36 and 41.

3. A sub-thesis of this chapter will thus be a concomitant questioning of the modern liturgical tendency to 'fix' the priest behind the altar in almost unvarying facial availability to the people; here, for contemporary Roman Catholicism in particular, the danger of a 'play-acting' of the Christ role, *qua* male, becomes extreme.

have found a deep point of contact and agreement. It is also to have located the source of the profound erotic passion that fuels the disagreement in the first place. Ecumenical advance can therefore only be achieved by attention to this nexus, not by avoidance.

Finally, in this introduction, let me admit an element of autobiography in the way this argument has developed, for it has implications for what might be called the epistemological underpinnings of the line of thought to be traced. I must own that I could scarcely have dreamed up this particular collection of ideas in advance of my own ordination to the priesthood (which happened now some time ago, in July 2001). I had already, to be sure, done a significant amount of research on the connection between prayer (especially contemplative prayer), eroticism, and the development of trinitarian doctrine in the patristic era.[4] So my scholarly work was already attuned to the problematic nexus of sexual desire and desire for God, a nexus that shows us, I believe, why communion with the divine always tends to summon the erotic metaphor. But my investigation of *liturgical*, and specifically eucharistic, prayer in this context had been regrettably slight.[5] It was only in learning

---

4. Some aspects of these themes are explored in a preliminary way in *Powers and Submissions: Philosophy, Spirituality and Gender* (Oxford: Blackwell, 2002), but are treated in more detail in the first volume of my systematics: *God, Sexuality and the Self: An Essay 'On the Trinity'* (Cambridge: Cambridge University Press, 2013), esp. ch. 3.

5. I discuss the trinitarian shape of eucharistic prayer briefly in 'Why Three? Some Further Reflections on the Origins of the Doctrine of the Trinity', in Sarah Coakley and David A. Pailin, eds, *The Making and*

to celebrate the eucharist myself, in immersing myself in something of the history of eucharistic enactment, and in so doing finding that I had to make a host of apparently minor choices nonetheless encoded with immense theological significance, that I began fully to appreciate the gender and erotic latency of the eucharistic act. Any new priest will be aware of the intensity of these choices. How to modulate one's gestures, whether to use manual acts (and if so, of what sort), how to dispose one's body in prayer, whether to elevate the elements, where in one's voice to pitch one's chanting: all these questions assumed for me levels of significance, both theological and in relation to my own sense of self as a woman, that could hardly be gainsaid, and went beyond mere consideration of the liturgical text and rubric into the more nebulous but intuitive category of ritual performance. Further decisions which were to affect not only my liturgical activity but my general life as a priest also impinged: what sort of clerical dress to choose, what shoes, whether to mix clerical collar and lay clothes, whether to wear any make-up or jewellery, how to wear one's hair – none of these decisions are without considerable impact on the nexus of themes described at the outset of this lecture, as any reflective priest will surely admit.

Such emerging insights in my case were intensified by my own rather odd arrangement of belonging, as an Anglican priest of the diocese of Oxford, to two very different parishes – one in England, one in North America – as well as to

Remaking of Christian Doctrine (Oxford: Oxford University Press, 1993), pp. 29–56, at 45.

an ecumenical Divinity School at Harvard. In the summer
I was at this time a curate at Littlemore, outside Oxford,
where John Henry Newman built the church before his sub-
sequent conversion to Rome, and fixed a stone altar inexorably into the East end so that perforce one celebrates with
one's back to the people.[6] I had expected to find this offensive as a feminist, but oddly – for reasons that will become
clearer as we proceed – I found it impinged on the gender
implications of the rite with surprisingly positive effect. In
my parish in Waban, Massachusetts, in contrast, and at Harvard Divinity School, different forms of celebration were in
use which for the most part keep the priest facing the people (except on high days and holy days at Waban, when one
circumambulated the altar to cense it). To these apparently
insignificant details I shall return in the last section of this
essay.

I mention these autobiographical asides now, however,
because they have bearing on the status of the truth claims
implied by what I am going to propose. Let us admit it: we
are in a realm of argument here where straightforward tex-
tual analysis, or strict rational logic, are unlikely to present
an obvious knock-down case. As anthropologists, ritual the-
orists, and psychoanalysts tend to know better than theologians, the evocations of gesture, bodily posture, vocal tone

---

6. The original stone altar and reredos of 1836, installed by Newman,
were later moved back to accommodate a choir and larger chancel: see
George F. Tull, *Littlemore: An Oxfordshire Village, Then and Now* (Rother-
ham: The King's England Press, 2002), pp. 17–27. Apparently Newman
himself, having opted for his contentiously 'Roman' stone altar, nonetheless celebrated 'North end', in traditional Anglican mode.

and sartorial choice can, as an accompaniment to a normative liturgical text, make (literally) all the difference in the
world. And indeed that is what is at stake, according to the
conservatives: a potential *cosmological* disturbance caused by
a woman at the altar. Making judgments about this realm
of (subliminal) evocation and (intuitive) reception is thus
notoriously tricky, and this we have to acknowledge at the
outset.[7] But that is why I propose, now, to proceed first by
means of interlocution with two eminent conservatives who
have already beaten these bounds with some care – the first
an anthropologist (Mary Douglas), the second a theologian
(Hans Urs von Balthasar). By meeting their arguments at
face value, and their data with honesty, we may hope to keep
our initial discussion as free as possible from charges of sub-
jective eisegesis. When we then turn in our last section to
some readings of the details of the liturgy which may seem
more hermeneutically contentious, we shall at least have the
'meat' of this earlier discussion to sustain us.

Two Interlocutors: Mary Douglas (1921–2007) and Hans Urs von Balthasar (1905–88)

To help me unfold my argument in more detail, then, let
me now invoke, albeit briefly, the positions of Douglas and
von Balthasar. As we shall see, their arguments have significant moves in common; and this is not surprising, given

---

7. This is not to say that I think such judgements are *impossible*; on the
contrary, as I hope to show, the truth conditions of an argument that
appeals – amongst other things – to the rather subtle lessons of liturgical performance *can* be displayed, discussed and duly adjudicated.

that the latter at least indirectly influenced the former. For Douglas takes the statements of the magisterium against the ordination of women (in whose production and defence Balthasar played an important role), as norm and starting point. However, despite the acknowledged hermeneutical circularity involved here, I think each author will illuminate the other. I shall advert first to the specifically anthropological considerations presented by Douglas, and then probe back behind her to the deeper theological complexities of Balthasar's position.

a. *Mary Douglas.* In an intriguing article entitled 'The Gender of the Beloved' published in a *Festschrift* volume for Robert Murray, S. J.,[8] Douglas provides her own, specifically anthropological, support (as well as significant suggestions for adjustment) to the 1976 Vatican statement against the ordination of women, *Inter Insigniores.* I turn to this article first because it is remarkably unambiguous, indeed wholly unembarrassed, about the gender binary on which its whole anthropological argument hinges; and yet in the course of its outworking, it seems, as I see it, to undo itself.

Starting with a citation of the 1976 Vatican statement, Douglas confirms her full agreement with its central insistence that 'the nuptial mystery sums up the way the Church has always seen her own identity'; and she does not baulk at the further conclusion (not obviously a *sequitur,* of course) that: 'A man is an exemplar of masculinity which enables the priest to represent Christ in the mystery of God made

8. Mary Douglas, 'The Gender of the Beloved,' *The Heythrop Journal* 36 (1995), 397–408.

man'.[9] Yet she admits that the 'controversy' over this view is 'hot with prejudice' since Vatican II; and that the conservative position of *Inter Insigniores* has a 'fusty' look, as she puts it, a form of teaching 'opportunistically brought out of the attic, still in dust wraps, and applied as a heavy bludgeon'.[10] So she suggests rejuvenating it a little with the aid of anthropological insights about 'natural signs', first, 'institutional identity', second, and 'sacred marriages', third. Let me say a word about each of these anthropological themes as treated by Douglas. For in my view, far from *supporting* the Vatican position, her evidence in at least two of the areas ('natural signs' and 'sacred marriages') seems rather to undermine it; and in the final theme that she treats ('institutional identity'), she not only provides a surprising *addendum* to the Vatican's proposals for women, but also leaves us, I suggest, with some fruitful lessons to take forward in the overall thesis of this paper.

First, on 'natural signs', so-called, Douglas rightly insists — *contra* the implied rhetoric of *Inter Insigniores* — that gender binaries cannot simply be supported by an appeal to their 'naturalness'. 'In the strict sense', she writes, 'there are no natural signs. The idea of nature is a cultural artefact. Talk about signs is talk about interpretation. Anything can be interpreted as a natural sign: if it is seen as such, then that sign has been naturalized in that culture'.[11] And thus, 'Signs are open; they [only] get a stable meaning *from the way they are*

9. Douglas, 'The Gender,' 397.

10. Douglas, 'The Gender,' 398.

11. Douglas, 'The Gender,' 399.

institutionalized ... In this case, the idea of the divine Bridegroom justifies the institution of male priesthood'.[12] But we
see that the cat is immediately out of the bag here; for if
indeed the supposed stability of 'nature' is a *chimera*, then no
amount of institutional 'freezing' of roles by appeal to such
a 'nature' can any longer impress us. Our signification is ever
fluid, ever re-made, ever open to new 'interpretation': such,
by Douglas's own admission, is the necessary conclusion of
anthropological insight. Her own proposal, then, that feminists must not *repress* the Bride-Bridegroom theme (she
only has *that* sort of 'feminist' in mind, unfortunately), but
must 'build on it to reformulate their universe',[13] given this
capacity for fluid signification, is, of course, precisely what I
too am after. So far so good.

Douglas's appeal, secondly, to the anthropological evidence on 'sacred marriage' is also telling. Again, she thinks
that the Congregation for the Doctrine of the Faith could
well learn from the anthropological guild. She points out
that the Vatican's attempt to provide evidence of straightforward continuity with biblical tradition on the nuptial
theme of Yahweh and Israel is flawed: in the Hebrew Scrip-
tures Israel is more often seen as the unfaithful and 'whor-
ing' wife or lover than an obedient spouse. Again, tradition
has been shown to be fluid, open, adventurous. Adverting to
erotic religious poetry beyond the bounds of Christianity,

---

12. Douglas, 'The Gender,' 399, my italics.

13. See Douglas, 'The Gender,' 398: 'We would do better to take the
nuptial mystery and run with it, not against it.'

Douglas admits (*vis-à-vis* Persian materials, for instance[14]), that the nuptial metaphor can be found in many weird and wonderful forms: 'the beloved can be male or female, God may be presented in a feminine role as the lost beloved whom the human soul (masculine) strives to reach. Or, the other way round, the feminine human soul may have been lost, captured or imprisoned, while the Lord God in masculine image overcomes formidable obstacles to reach and rescue her. Sometimes the gender of the beloved switches, sometimes God is a masculine and sometimes a feminine principle'.[15] Such, again, seems to be the lesson of anthropology, that fixity of gender roles in the realm of erotic/divine poetry is the exception, not the rule. Had Douglas explored a little more deeply *within* Christian tradition, of course, the same trait could be shown (especially in celebrated commentaries on the Song of Songs[16]); but her conclusions are oddly blunt: she seems to think that the modern 'feminist' demands the direct inversion of gender binaries, rather than their more subtle *subversion*. Again, as I see it, she fails to

---

14. See Douglas, 'The Gender,' 402, and 408 n. 4, which thanks Aditya Behl for information on gender fluidity in Persian materials from his research on 'Gender Politics in the Madhumalati.'

15. Douglas, 'The Gender,' 402.

16. Such capacity for gender transformation (both in humanity and in anthropomorphic attributions to God) is a striking feature of the *Commentary on the Song of Songs* by the late fourth-century Greek patristic author, Gregory of Nyssa (of whom more will be said below, in relation to his influence on von Balthasar's thought). For a short introduction to this theme in Nyssen, see Sarah Coakley, ed., *Re-Thinking Gregory of Nyssa* (Oxford: Blackwell, 2003) 1–13.

draw the conclusion that her own summoning of anthropological evidence has tantalizingly suggested. Why, then, does Douglas still support the view of the Vatican? It is partly, to be sure, that she has negatively pigeon-holed the 'feminist' cause in a way that finds it guilty of repressive instincts and an egalitarianism that flattens gender difference; but here I am on Douglas's side, not that of her presumed 'feminist' opponents. It is really her third area of anthropological discussion, then, that of 'institutional identity' that is key for her. And here she produces her own particular defence of 'hierarchy', familiar from her other later writings,[17] which insists that 'hierarchy' is a form of social organization that women should actually welcome, since it protects all its members, including the weakest – often, of course, in less developed societies, women themselves. And since the Roman Catholic church is an inherently 'hierarchical' institution, she says, it is more realistic to try and *reform* its hierarchical arrangements than to insist that it become something else. Better, then, according to Douglas (and here is her unexpected *novum*), to insist that the Vatican set up a powerful commission for women's issues, equivalent in its balancing influence within the hierarchy to that wielded by the Queen Mother in certain African societies, than that women – falsely driven by flattening *egalitarian* aims – should seek to repress the nuptial metaphor for the

---

17. See, for instance, the more extensive discussions of 'hierarchy' in Mary Douglas, 'Thought Styles Exemplified: The Idea of the Self', in *Risk and Blame* (London: Routledge, 1992), pp. 211–34; and eadem, *Thought Styles* (London: Sage Publications, 1996).

priesthood and so topple the ban on women's ordination.[18]
Now this is altogether an odd and unexpected argument,
as may be agreed. Douglas nowhere satisfactorily faces head-
on her remaining commitment as a conservative Catholic
to the gender-binary of priest/'male' and church/'female',[19]
since much of the anthropological evidence she supplies
along the way would appear to help undermine it. But her
remarks about *falsely* egalitarian feminism, and the compar-
ative merits of *some* forms of 'institutional hierarchy', are
in my view not without point. Since any church that has a
priesthood and an episcopacy is inherently 'hierarchical' in
Douglas's generic anthropological sense, it is as well to drop
the dismissive critique of 'hierarchy' *tout court*, and concentrate instead on imagining the possibility of a priestly hierarchy where gender binaries are *not* fixed in the way that *Inter Insigniores* would have us believe is inevitable. That indeed
is the rub. And as we have seen, Douglas's analysis almost *en
passant*, and in spite of itself, gives reasons for suggesting
that option to be anthropologically possible. Let us now see
how our second, and arguably more formidable, conservative interlocutor, von Balthasar, adds some profound theological considerations to this picture, before moving to our
constructive suggestion.

---

18. See Douglas, 'The Gender,' 406–8.

19. 'Male'/'masculine' (and likewise 'female'/'feminine') are crucially
conflated in Douglas, as they are also in von Balthasar. Hence no critical
attempt is made by either author to discuss the relation of physiological morphology to (shifting) cultural stereotypes about gender. This
matter is of course highly contentious in contemporary gender theory.

b. *Hans Urs von Balthasar.* The extraordinary richness and complexity of Balthasar's theory of gender has still not received the detailed analysis it deserves. To read, say, his short *Mysterium Paschale* (alone), as many in the English-speaking world do, is to miss completely the gender evocations with which his kenotic trinitarian theology of the cross is larded elsewhere (most notably in his *Theodramatik*)[20]. Gender is so profoundly woven into his deepest theological themes (Trinity, Christology, ecclesiology, Mariology), and so surprisingly and counter-intuitively in some of its twists and turns, that I cannot possibly do full justice to its entanglement with the issue of priestly status in this brief treatment.

20. Compare Hans Urs von Balthasar, *Mysterium Pascale* (Edinburgh: T. & T. Clark, 1990) – a text originally written at speed for an encyclopaedia volume, and strikingly devoid of gender allusions – with *Theo-drama* (San Francisco: Ignatius Press, 1988–), especially volumes 3 (1992) and 4 (1994), which are replete with gender themes. In the brief treatment of gender in von Balthasar that follows I must express my grateful reliance on the feminist analysis of this theme in an unpublished Harvard M. Div Senior Thesis by Margaret Marshall, 'Figures of the Feminine: Symbolics of Gender in the Christology of Hans Urs von Balthasar', Harvard Divinity School, Spring 2000. A doctoral dissertation written at the same time at the Gregorian gives, by contrast, an exhaustive, but entirely adulatory, account of von Balthasar's views on gender and the priesthood: Robert A. Pesarchick, *The Trinitarian Foundation of Human Sexuality As Revealed by Christ According to Hans Urs von Balthasar: The Revelatory Significance of the Male Christ and the Male Ministerial Priesthood* (Rome: Editrice Pontificia Universita Gregoriana, 2000). With these compare the more recent essays by Rowan Williams, 'Balthasar and the Trinity', and Corinne Crammer, 'One sex or two? Balthasar's theology of the sexes', in Edward T. Oakes, S. J. and David Moss, eds, *The Cambridge Companion to Hans Urs von Balthasar* (Cambridge: Cambridge University Press, 2004), pp. 37–50 and 93–112.

I shall simply fasten for these present purposes on three central points of analysis, which together will provide us with a fulcrum for critical discussion. I shall turn, first, to the central issue of his rejection of the ordination of women, and his ostensible reasons for it; and then, secondly, to his accompanying Mariology, as the crucial focus for his reflection on the church as 'feminine'; and then, finally, to the complexity of his gender-theorizing on the Trinity, a place where – I shall argue – the influence of his work on Gregory of Nyssa shines through, with its strong hint of a possibility of gender transformation as a continuing condition of the life of incorporation into God.[21] As with Mary Douglas's anthropological work, then, so too here: I find a stern argument for the cosmological *impossibility* of women's priestly sacramental ministry *combined with* the very potential for that argument's undoing. To our three tasks we go briefly in turn, then.

At the heart, first, of Balthasar's explicit rejection of the ordination of women is a key paradox, which simultaneously reveals a *capacity* for 'fluid' thinking about gender *vis-à-vis* men, and yet a means of 'fixing' womanhood outside the bounds of priesthood. It is well expressed in the essay he wrote as commentary on the publication of *Inter Insigniores*, entitled 'The Uninterrupted Tradition of the Church', and also in a later essay 'Women Priests?' in *New Elucidations.*[22]

---

21. See Hans Urs von Balthasar, *Presence and Thought: An Essay on the Religious Philosophy of Gregory of Nyssa* (San Francisco: Ignatius Press, 1995). The original French edition was published in 1988.

22. Hans Urs von Balthasar, 'The Uninterrupted Tradition of the

On the one hand, men and women are 'equal', and nowhere is this clearer than in the person of Christ: as Balthasar puts it in the latter essay, 'One can say that Christ, inasmuch as he represents the God of the universe in the world, is likewise the origin of both feminine and masculine principles in the church ...'[23] Yet this equality does not suppress a 'difference' which is even more fundamental: 'the Catholic Church is perhaps humanity's last bulwark of genuine appreciation of the *difference* of the sexes', he writes, and of 'the extreme oppositeness of their functions ...'[24] It is actually the 'feminine' which for Balthasar is seen as primary for the Church, and pedestalized as the 'comprehensive feminine, the marian', unsullied and actively 'fruitful', 'already *superior* to that of the man';[25] and yet it is the man, 'consecrated into [his] office' who *alone* can represent the 'specifically masculine function – the transmission of a vital force that originates outside itself and leads beyond itself'.[26] As Balthasar puts it in a much-quoted remark in another essay: 'What else is his Eucharist but, at a higher level, an endless act of fruitful outpouring of his whole flesh, such as a man can only achieve for a moment with a limited organ of his body?'[27]

Church', in *From 'Inter Insigniores' to 'Ordinatio Sacerdotalis'*, pp. 99–106; and Hans Urs von Balthasar, 'Women Priests?', in *New Elucidations* (San Francisco: Ignatius Press, 1986), pp. 187–98 .

23. von Balthasar, 'Women Priests?', p. 193.

24. von Balthasar, 'Women Priests?', p. 195.

25. von Balthasar, 'Women Priests?', pp. 193, 192.

26. von Balthasar, 'Women Priests?', p. 193.

27. Hans Urs von Balthasar, *Elucidations* (London: SPCK, 1975), p. 150.

So here we confront the essential gender double-think at the heart of Balthasar's system: the priest *must* be physiologically male, though also 'feminine' *qua* transmitter of an ecclesial vital force that is more fundamentally that of the 'perfect feminine Church.'[28] Women, however, are always and *only* 'feminine', expressing their 'natural fruitfulness' which is 'already superior to that of the man':[29] 'equal' but 'different', 'equal' but *superior* (even), but 'equal' and inherently and physiologically incapable of the priesthood. As Balthasar puts it triumphantly in 'The Uninterrupted Tradition', alluding to Ephesians 5, 'The redemptive mystery "Christ-Church" is the superabundant fulfilment of the mystery of creation between man and woman . . . The natural difference is charged, *as* difference, with a supernatural emphasis . . .' Only this nuptial model can reflect the 'decisive light about the real reciprocity between the man and woman.'[30] Thus if a woman aspires to be a priest, she is disordered, breaking the rules of her own primary 'fruitfulness'.

This central paradox — all are 'equal', but men are more equal than women (to adapt a phrase of Orwell) — is reduplicated, secondly, in the Marian fundament that sustains it. For whilst the 'feminine' here, as Mary, is the *sine qua non* of the church (as Balthasar puts it, 'The Church begins with the Yes of the Virgin of Nazareth'[31]), this 'feminine' tips over into petrine 'masculinity' *where men are concerned*: 'What

28. von Balthasar, 'Women Priests?', p. 193.

29. von Balthasar, 'Women Priests?', p. 192.

30. von Balthasar, 'The Uninterrupted Tradition', p. 101.

31. von Balthasar, 'Women Priests?', p. 192.

Peter will receive as "infallibility" for his office of governing will be a partial share in the total flawlessness of the feminine, marian church,' he writes.[32] Thus a fluidity from and between 'femininity' and 'masculinity' is the lot of the man, whilst, in contrast, woman is only and solely the 'feminine', a conclusion that Balthasar however roundly denies signifies a 'precedence' for the man: 'Who has precedence in the end? The man bearing office, inasmuch as he represents Christ in and before the community, or the woman, in whom the nature of the church is embodied — so much so that every member of the Church, *even the priest*, must maintain a feminine receptivity to the Lord of the Church? This question is completely idle, for the difference ought only to serve the mutual love of all the members in a circulation over which God alone remains sublimely supreme.'[33]

If we ask, finally, how this (selective) potential for gender fluidity finds its counterpart in Balthasar's thought about God-as-Trinity, we confront even more fascinating and labile material. As a careful reading of the *Theodramatik* in particular shows,[34] Balthasar can re-apply his theory of 'femininity' and 'masculinity' at this higher level of reflection to arrive at the following conundrum: that the Son is 'feminine'

---

32. von Balthasar, 'Women Priests?', p. 193.

33. von Balthasar, 'Women Priests?', pp. 197–8.

34. Here I follow the analysis of von Balthasar's gender themes in relation to the Trinity as explicated by Marshall, 'Figures of the Feminine', 13–14. See especially von Balthasar, *Theo-drama* V, p. 91, for the reciprocity of gender in the Trinity. Also see Rowan Williams's discussion of the same topic in 'Balthasar and the Trinity'.

in relation to the Father's 'masculinity', yet Father *and* Son are 'masculine' in jointly spirating the (initially 'feminine') Spirit; and yet again that the Father too can be said to be 'feminine' in receiving the processions back into himself from the other two. All the persons, in other words, are *both* 'masculine' and 'feminine'; and by extension, it must be again that the Christ/Word/priest who 'pours himself out' as seed at the altar is *also* 'feminine', receptive, as representing the capacity of the church so to be fructified.

And so we arrive at what I suggest is the internal undoing of Balthasar's own recitation of gender binaries. For while the woman is fixed normatively as 'feminine', both pedestalized and subordinated (though not in rhetoric, as we have seen), the male in contrast has this infinite capacity for reversal and internal reciprocity, just as God's 'persons' do. It is as if the profound influence on Balthasar of Gregory of Nyssa's subversive gender fluidity, so fascinatingly expressed in Gregory's ascetic works and in his commentary on the Song of Songs,[35] here meets and is stopped short *in the woman's case* by Balthasar's immovable German romanticism, his adulation of *das ewig Weibliche*. It is an odd, fascinating, and altogether uncomfortable mix, as I hope these brief foci for examination have shown. But it is a mix concocted, however oddly, from two quite different inheritances of the primary symbolism of the nuptial metaphor.

Let us now consider finally, then, what this all might mean for our contemporary consideration of gender and eucha-

---

35. See von Balthasar's own discussion of these themes in his *Presence and Thought*, pp. 153–61.

ristic priestly enactment, and its continuing connection with that erotic metaphor.

The Woman at the Altar: Beating the Bounds of Gender Liminality

I said at the start of this chapter that I was set on demonstrating that the priest is in 'an inherently fluid gender role as beater of the liminal bounds between the divine and the human'. Perhaps we are now in a better position, after our interlocutions with Douglas and Balthasar, to argue this more fully in closing. For what I hope these two interrogations have shown is that neither author can finally account for the reason for 'fixing' the priest as 'male'/'masculine', when the very material they survey, whether anthropological or theological, inherently presses them towards a creative destabilizing of the gender binaries they valorize. They could, of course (and here comes a final twist to my argument), present a devious *riposte* to this critique which neither, interestingly, considers, *viz.*, that the eucharist has always represented an artful 'ritual of *reversal*' (an instantiation of gender fluidity in the *male* priest) that covertly re-establishes the norm of 'appropriate' gender distribution which is its *opposite*. That, indeed, might be my own anthropological comment on what may have been occurring, implicitly, in the Christian centuries during which only men have been ordained: the exception has indeed proved the 'rule'. But that does not prevent us from pressing on with our own line of analysis, and asking now more pointedly in this last section our crucial contemporary question: If an acknowledgement of the significance of the nuptial metaphor calls forth an awareness of the erotic aura of the priest's mediating of the boundary between the divine and the human, then wherein lies the distribution of the 'natural' signs (in Douglas's anthropological terms) of 'masculinity' and 'femininity' in the priest's negotiation of this boundary?[36] And what difference is made to the liturgical perception of this negotiation if the priest can be female as well as male?

My answer to this will involve picking up some strands

---

36. By now it may be clear that the 'binary' of divine/human needs rather careful distinction from the *gender* 'binary' of 'masculine'/'feminine' (since *different* understandings of 'difference' are at stake). The conservative position, as we have shown at some length, sees the latter as irreducibly, and immovably, connected to the former as a 'natural' sign, and the eucharist as liturgically performing this supposedly immovable given of gender difference. My view, in contrast, is that while the *first* 'binary' of 'difference' (of transcendent divine gift and human response) must always be summoned and 're-presented' in the eucharist, its effect – rightly understood – is actually one of de-stabilizing and transforming static societal gender roles: there is *alteration*, no 're-fixing', of gender as a result. The 'world' is disturbed and transformed. Thus there is a paradox here: the 'erotic' metaphor for the eucharist *is* still irreducible and ontologically basic (because founded in the divine *eros* for the human); but its irreducibility does not reside in its leaving gender *as it is*. One might say that its normativity consists in the way it *subverts* such 'normativity' at the human level.

From this it follows that my use in this essay of the metaphor of 'beating the bounds' of gender is also playful and paradoxical. Normally 'bounds' are 'beaten' in order to re-establish a clear *demarcation* between territories. But in my view, the priest at the *limen* between the divine and the human is 're-presenting' a *transgression* of the boundary between the human and the divine that occurs, transformatively, in the incarnation, and is found to have implications, too, for the transformation of static gender binaries.

from the autobiographical asides at the start of this chapter, and pointing to three dimensions of priestly eucharistic enactment which may not always *obviously* convey messages about gender, but in my view subliminally are doing so. My conclusion, to anticipate, will be that the woman's presence as priest in these negotiations makes it impossible any more to count these gender destabilizations as reversals that merely prove the patriarchal 'rule'. Rather, these destabilizations can now be seen as *endemic* to the life of transformation into God to which the eucharist invites us. Let me explain a little further with my three chosen liturgical examples.

First, recall my remark that I was startled to discover, in celebrating East-facing at Littlemore, that far from finding myself offended by this position as a feminist,[37] I actually found the East-position curiously releasing. I think I can now give a theological account of this, as follows. When the priest has her back to the people, it is symbolically clear that she is adopting the position of 'offering' on behalf *of* the laity: she is facing Godwards, representing the *laos*. In the terms of the old 'natural signs' (which, as Mary Douglas argues, cannot be repressively obliterated, but must rather – in my view – be re-summoned and strategically destabilized), the priest is 'feminine' in this posture – supremely Marian, as Balthasar would see it. But when she turns around, whether to greet (at the *sursum corda*), or to offer the consecrated elements, or to bless, she has moved to the other side of the divide,

---

37. The classic feminist case *against* 'hierarchy' and East-facing celebration may be found in Nancy Jay, *Throughout Your Generations Forever* (Chicago: University of Chicago Press, 1992).

representing Christ, offering God *to* the people – again, in the terms of the nuptial metaphor, both summoning and destabilizing the 'masculine' posture of the bridegroom's self-gift. Without these bodily reversals and movements in the liturgy, I suggest, something deeply significant to the enactment of this destabilization is lost. When I am stuck, fixed behind the altar West-facing throughout, I also contribute unwittingly to a gender-fixing that blocks the play of liminality those older movements conveyed. As I suggested at the outset, it is not – and never was – that the priest *only* represented Christ, and the people *only* the church. Rather, by moving from one role and its evocations to the other, even the male priest 'played' with a destabilization of associated gender binaries. What the female priest now makes impossible, in my view, in her same play of movements, is the use of this play as a reversal that merely re-establishes its opposite; *her* destabilization is more confounding even than a 'ritual of reversal', and so gestures to the endlessness of the movement of gender subversion at the gateway between the divine and the human.

Such a claim is bold, I am aware; but I have a second, related, reflection about the dangers of a fixed Western-facing pose, and it is one I share with Orthodox commentators such as (most recently) Kallistos Ware, in an essay charting his change of mind on the question of women's ordination to an open-minded and potentially positive one.[38] It is that the Western-facing 'stuck' position, along with the manual

---

38. Kallistos Ware, 'Man, Woman and the Priesthood of Christ,' in Hopko, ed., *Women and the Priesthood*, pp. 5–53, at pp. 47–9.

acts that often attend it, unnecessarily intensifies the visu-
ally 'iconic' dimension of the priest's role as being *in persona
Christi*; the problem then may arise for the congregation that
this person's appearance (old, young, male, female, blonde,
bespectacled, spotty) seems incongruous as 'representative'
of Christ. What again is lost here is the capacity for labile
'play' over which way is being 'faced' — towards God or towards the church — and thus which gender association con-
comitantly summoned and queried.

My third and last liturgical focus I take from a fascinating — albeit speculative — analysis in a doctoral dissertation
by Ludger Viefhues,[39] of the implicit gender significance of
the censing of the altar at the offertory at High Mass. The
full details I cannot here unfold, for the argument involves
a complicated theory of the 'overlaying of contrasts' in the
ritual of the mass that Viefhues takes in part from the work
of the ritual theorist Catherine Bell.[40] His fundamental argument, however, is that the movement of the priest and
his/her assistants around the altar, and the concomitant
censing (which is both up and down and side to side, thus
summoning notions both of transcendent intervention and
of horizontal solidarity), is simultaneously establishing a
close association between the priest and the altar, as locus

39. Ludger Viefhues, 'Cavell, the Skeptic and The Diva: The Human Self
Between Gender and Transcendence,' Ph.D Thesis, Harvard University,
December 2001, at pp. 289–91.

40. See again Catherine Bell, *Ritual Theory, Ritual Practice* (New York:
Oxford University Press, 1992), a book that draws strongly — though
not uncritically — on the work of the French anthropologist Pierre
Bourdieu.

of vertical divine presence, but also simultaneously destabilizing such an association by the subordination of the priest to the divine centre of action on the altar and on the people, also indicated by the horizontal movements of the censing. That priestly gender associations are also here subliminally being both enacted and destabilized is part of Viefhues's argument: the 'traditional' hierarchy of gender (here: male God over female church), he suggests, is implicitly summoned but also dissolved, just as the ritual power of the priest is both enacted and subordinated through the complex movements of the censing.

Conclusions

Let me now sum up what I have, and have not, been arguing in this chapter. I set out to explore the classic gender associations of the nuptial metaphor for the eucharist, and argued that rather than repressing and rejecting this 'erotic' theological zone, we would do well to explore its fullest implications. In the course of an interrogation of Mary Douglas's and Hans Urs von Balthasar's reasons for the rejection of women priests, I argued that their own very insights pointed to an internal critique: the logic of the nuptial metaphor's outworking leads to a priestly destabilization of normative gender binaries rather than the opposite. However, the 'fixing' or 'freezing' back of such binaries, which has classically attended the liturgical play in destabilizing them, becomes, I argued, impossible once a real-life woman is at the altar; in that sense, we must indeed conclude that her presence represents a cosmological disturbance, in the original terms of the debate. It is not just that she is a woman dressing up as a man dressing up as a woman (though sartorial details are certainly significant in this 'play'), but rather that the gender fluidity that the male priest has always enjoyed *qua* liturgically liminal can no longer be a means of 'leaving *everything else* as it is'. Offensive as this logic must inevitably be to conservatives, whether Roman Catholic, Anglo-Catholic or Orthodox, it has the merit of meeting such opponents in their own chosen zone of nuptial reflection and working relentlessly through to the end that that theology suggests. If I am right, then the sort of perpetual destabilization of gender binaries that Nyssen glimpsed in his last writings is what that spiritual 'end' may be.

Finally, it should be noted that this argument presumes nothing about the sexual *orientation* of the priest who may become newly aware of this liturgical logic – though I have to admit that in my experience gay, lesbian or transgendered people are inclined to have a quicker understanding and sympathy for the form of logic I have unfolded here than are others. But I want to make it clear that this argument is not in any way an incitement to accentuate one's own sexual identity as a priest in the course of the liturgy (whether as gay or straight: such advertised self-reference would be a distraction); but nor is it a demand to *erase* gender. Rather, it is a matter of a subtly kenotic dispossession, a rendering of oneself prayerfully diaphanous to the fluidity of the *proto*-erotic dimensions of the divine nuptial enactment that one is 're-presenting'.[41] That is why this proposal

41. My use of the neologism 'proto-erotic' may require some brief ex-

is not at all the same as that of an old-style liberal 'androgyny', in which stereotypical 'feminine' and 'masculine' were
simply conjoined without critique ('like John Wayne and
Brigitte Bardot scotch-taped together', as Mary Daly once
caustically put it[42]); but nor is it the invitation to an explicit
priestly 'acting out' of a queer protest against gender stability, such as Judith Butler would enjoin.[43] It is something more

planation here at the close. This essay has been written on the metaphysical presumption that it is *divine* love and desire for the created
order ('proto-erotic' love) which is manifested at the incarnation, and
so at the eucharist, and which is also the ultimate source and cause of
the responsive human desire for the divine. What I here call 'the divine
nuptial enactment' is that incarnational flow of the divine to the human
and the enabling thereby of the human response. What the priest does,
and does *well* when appropriately and prayerfully disposed (that is, propelled by the grace of the Holy Spirit), is to allow the incarnational
impact of this flow of divine desire to be made manifest through a playful 're-presentation' of both symbolic poles – Christ and the church –
whilst implicitly questioning the 'normative' identification of one with
'masculinity' and the other with 'femininity'.

42. See Mary Daly, 'the qualitative leap beyond patriarchal religion', *Quest*
1.4 (1975), 20–40, at 30.

43. See especially Judith Butler, *Gender Trouble: Feminism and the Subversion
of Identity* (New York: Routledge, 1990). I have given a critical account
of Butler's gender theory from a specifically Christian theological perspective in my *Powers and Submissions*, pp. 153–67. It may be clear that
the view of gender that accompanies (and indeed arises from) the
theology of the eucharist proposed in this essay, does not belong on
either of the battle-lines in current secular gender theory (the physiological 'essentialisms' of the French feminists and the pragmatic gender
de-stabilizations of American 'queer theory'). That it escapes through
the horns of this particular dilemma is arguably a sign of its specifically
Christian and incarnational provenance: the transformation of gender
is a *divine* – but also an embodied – event, according to this view.

subtle than these secular theories can presume, precisely because it happens on the *limen* between the divine and the human, where the miracle of divine enfleshment challenges and undercuts the rigid orderings of the world. What I have laid before you in this reflection, then, should not be seen as a proposal about sexual ethics, as such, but rather a theory about that mysterious liminality of priestly enactment, a liminality that can through God's grace be a point of both mediation and transformation, a disturbing re-making, indeed, of the order of the world — both cosmological and personal. Insofar as the world *is* thus re-ordered, we know that the Spirit has broken in, and the Word made flesh; for what, after all, is the Incarnation itself, if not the greatest 'cosmological disturbance' that the 'world' has known?

3

LIVING INTO THE MYSTERY
OF THE HOLY TRINITY:
THE TRINITY, PRAYER AND SEXUALITY

IN THIS CHAPTER, I WANT TO LAY BEFORE YOU THREE theses about the Trinity that have much exercised me in my theological research over many years now, and which are, I believe, intertwined in a complex and fascinating way.[1] They relate to what I see as the interlocked themes of the Trinity, prayer and sexuality. Let me start with a succinct enunciation of my three theses, and then proceed to a slightly more ramified explication of each.

I. The first thesis is this: *that the revival of a vibrant trinitarian conceptuality, an 'earthed' sense of the meaningfulness and truth of the Christian doctrine of the Trinity, most naturally arises out of a simultaneous renewal of commitment to prayer, and especially prayer of a relatively wordless kind.* I shall try to explain why I think this is so with special reference to Paul's

---

1. For early explorations of these themes, see Sarah Coakley, 'Can God be Experienced as Trinity?', *The Modern Churchman* 28 (1986), 11–23; and eadem, 'Why Three? Some Further Reflections on the Doctrine of the Trinity', in eds Sarah Coakley and David A. Pailin, *The Making and Remaking of Christian Doctrine: Essays in Honour of Maurice Wiles* (Oxford: Oxford University Press, 1993), pp. 29–56. My fully developed account is now to be found in eadem, *God, Sexuality and the Self: An Essay 'On the Trinity'* (Cambridge: Cambridge University Press, 2013), esp. ch. 3.

discussion of the nature of Christian prayer in Romans 8 as 'sighs too deep for words' (Rom. 8.26), instituted by the Holy Spirit; and how I think this Spirit-led approach to the Trinity through prayer is the only experientially rooted one likely to provide some answer to the sceptical charge: why three 'persons' at all? Why believe in a trinitarian God in the first place?

So that will be my first thesis: the inextricability of renewed trinitarian conceptuality and the renewal of prayer-practice, and I shall be arguing that Christian prayer practice is inherently trinitarian.

II. The second thesis leads on from this, and is perhaps a little more surprising; it is that *the close analysis of such prayer, and its implicitly trinitarian structure, makes the confrontation of a particular range of fundamental issues about sexuality unavoidable.* (Note that I use 'sexuality' in a wider sense than it is often employed, especially in North America: I am not restricting it to actual genital sexual activity.) The unavoidability of this confrontation seems to me to arise from the profound entanglement of our human sexual desires and our desire for God; and in any prayer of the sort in which we radically cede control to the Spirit there is an instant reminder of the close analogue between this ceding (to the trinitarian God), and the *ekstasis* of human sexual passion. Thus it is not a coincidence that intimate relationship is at the heart of both these matters. The early Fathers were aware of this nexus of associations between trinitarian conceptuality, deep prayer, and the connections with issues of sex and gender that to them seemed dangerous.

I shall illustrate this with a particular example from the third-century Alexandrian theologian, Origen. What will emerge from this second thesis, I hope, is that no renewed trinitarian spirituality can *sidestep* these profound issues of the nature of sexual desire, issues which now so divisively exercise us in the Church's life, and are, in turn, of course, fundamentally connected with gender themes about women's roles, women's capacity for empowerment, and for professional equality.

In short, it is not a coincidence that the quest for renewed spiritual practice, for enlivened trinitarian doctrine, and for an honest confrontation of tough questions in the contemporary Church about issues of sexuality and gender, coincide. For these three issues all belong together, and can be shown with a bit of delicate archaeological digging beneath the polite edifice constructed by the standard textbooks in the history of doctrine, to have accompanied one another all along. Or so I shall argue.

III. My third thesis, then finally, is not so much a finished proposition, but a task in progress for us all. It is the task of *rethreading the strands of inherited tradition on these three matters in such a way that enacted sexual desire and desire for God are no longer seen in mutual enmity, as disjunctive alternatives, with the non-celibate woman or homosexual cast as the distractor from the divine goal.* Rather, we are seeking a renewed vision of divine desire (a trinitarian vision, I suggest) which may provide the guiding framework for a renewed theology of human sexuality – of godly sexual relations – rooted in, and *in some sense* analogously related to, trinitarian divine relations.

There are no short cuts here, and certainly no easy ways to conceive of creaturely participation in the life of the Trinity without a profound acknowledgement of the realities of sin and of the ongoing need for transformation and purification. But again, I want to suggest, there are resources in the tradition for this new task of reflection, even if one has to dig a bit.

Now this is rather a lot to tackle in one short chapter! But let me say at least a bit more about these three theses in turn, and where my research and thinking have led me.

I. *The Trinity in prayer-practice.* Why was the perfect relationship in God understood as triadic in the first place? I want to argue that an analysis of Christian prayer (especially relatively-wordless contemplative or charismatic prayer) provides an acutely revealing matrix for explaining the origins of trinitarian reflection. Vital here is Paul's analysis of prayer in Romans 8, where he describes how, strictly speaking, we do not autonomously do the praying, for we do not even really know what to ask for; rather it is the 'Spirit' who prays in us to the ultimate source in God ('the Father', or 'Abba') and does so with 'sighs too deep for words' that transcend normal human rationality.[2] Into that ceaseless divine

---

2. I do not here address the vexed issue of whether a feminist theologian should, under any circumstances, call God 'Father'. In *God, Sexuality and the Self*, ch. 7, I argue that in *inner-trinitarian* contexts there are theological reasons why it is difficult to insist on consistent substitutions for 'Father' language: 'creator', 'redeemer' and 'sanctifier', for instance, do not do the same theological *work* as 'Father', 'Son' and 'Holy Spirit'. In addition, the attempt to repress *all* 'Father' language out of liturgical usage may merely force paternal imagery underground, leaving it to

dialogue between Spirit and 'Father' the Christian pray-er is thus caught up, and so transformed, becoming a co-heir with Christ and being fashioned into an extension of redeemed, incarnate life. Recall how Paul puts it:

> For all who are led by the Spirit of God are sons of God. For you did not receive a spirit of slavery to fall back into fear, but you have received a spirit of adoption. When we cry, 'Abba, Father!' it is that very Spirit bearing witness with our spirit that we are children of God, and if children, then heirs of God and joint heirs with Christ ... Likewise the Spirit helps us in our weakness; for we do not know how to pray as we ought, but that very Spirit intercedes with sighs too deep for words. And God, who searches the heart, knows what is the mind of the Spirit, because the Spirit intercedes for the saints according to the will of God. (Rom. 8.14–17a, 26–7)

It is important to underscore that what is going on here is not three distinguishable types of 'experience' (in the sense of emotional tonality), each experience relating to a different point of identity – 'Father', 'Son' and 'Holy Spirit'. This, in any case, would prove to be a 'hunting of the snark' from the perspective of later developed orthodox trinitarianism, since the *homoousion* principle disallows that the different

---

continue its (often baleful) effects out of conscious sight. My solution is a multi-pronged one, including the use of deliberate illogical conjunction (maternal and paternal imagery combined) as a means of avoiding crass literalism in the attribution of parental characteristics; but the most important response to this problem is itself an ascetic task for us all (a matter of transformation of consciousness, meaning-association and healing via the practices of prayer), rather than a quick semantic 'fix' by *fiat*.

'persons' should be experientially separate, or do different things. Rather, what is being described by Paul is *one* experience of an activity of prayer that is nonetheless ineluctably, though obscurely, triadic. It is *one* experience of God, but God as simultaneously (i) doing the praying in me, (ii) receiving that prayer, and (iii) in that exchange, consented to in me, inviting me into the Christic life of redeemed sonship. Or to put it another way: the 'Father' (so-called here) is both source and ultimate object of divine longing in us; the 'Spirit' is that irreducibly, though obscurely, distinct enabler and incorporator of that longing in creation (that which *makes* the creation divine); and the 'Son' is that divine and perfected creation, into whose life I, as pray-er, am caught up. In this sense, despite all the unclarity and doctrinal fuzziness of Romans 8, the prayer described here seems to be at least 'proto-trinitarian' in its implications.

Now no-one would suggest that most of our prayer, sweated out as it so often is in states of dryness and distraction, may clearly feel like this. But just occasionally, I submit, if we allow enough space in which we are not insistently setting the agenda – if we allow, that is, this precious *hiatus* for the Spirit – then we breathe the Spirit's breath in this way. We see briefly that this is, theologically speaking, the triadic structure of God's graced ways with us, what is always going on though we mostly cannot see it. As John of the Cross puts it, not coincidentally quoting Romans 8 (and the cognate Galatians 4.4): 'By his divine breath-like spiration, the Holy Spirit elevates the soul sublimely and informs her and makes her capable of breathing in God the same spiration of love that the Father breathes in the Son and the Son in the Father.'[3]

The Spirit, on this view, is no redundant third, no hypostatized afterthought, no cooing 'feminine' adjunct to an established male household. Rather, experientially speaking, the Spirit is *primary*, just as Pentecost is primary for the Church; and leaving non-cluttered space for the Spirit is the absolute precondition for the unimpeded flowing of this divine exchange in us, the 'breathing of the divine breath', as John of the Cross puts it.

Now what we want to know next is this (and it brings us to our second thesis): What happened to exegesis of Romans 8 in the critical early patristic period? Why was it not the wellspring of the turbulent conciliar discussion of the Trinity? And why, as it seems from the standard textbooks, did the Spirit get properly attended to only third and last (in the later fourth century) in the development of trinitarian doctrine in the crucial early patristic period, when the equality of the rational Logos with the 'Father' was discussed and established so much earlier? Or was this really so? Was there perhaps a 'soft underbelly' to the history of the development of trinitarian doctrine that the textbooks have obscured, in which the Spirit played a much more significant role from the outset?

II. *The Trinity and sexuality.* My answer to this last question, although it is a speculative answer, is 'Yes'. There *is* a 'soft underbelly' to the history of the early development of the doctrine of the Trinity which the Fathers had reason to push

---

3. *The Spiritual Canticle* 39.3, in *John of the Cross: Selected Writings*, ed. Kieran Kavanaugh (New York: Paulist Press, 1987), p. 280.

to one side. What I suggest is that there is an alternative account of the genealogy of the doctrine which only becomes clear once we see the covert entanglement of this genealogy with questions of (what we now call) 'sex' and 'gender'.

What is striking, first, is how little Romans 8 gets used as a basis for trinitarian argument and reflection in the early period, admitting some important exceptions in Irenaeus, Origen, and then the later Athanasius.[4] My hypothesis is that this is because this Romans 8 approach, fertile as it was theologically, proved a little too hot to handle. Why?

What I suggest here is that, from the second century on, there were both politico-ecclesiastical *and* gender reasons for keeping this approach to the Trinity away from the centre stage in the public conciliar discussions of the matter. For Paul's analysis of prayer in Romans 8 notably involves: (i) a certain loss of noetic control to the leading experiential force of the Spirit in the face of our weakness (8.26); (ii) an entry into a realm beyond words, beyond normal rationality or *logos* (ibid.); and (iii) the striking use of a (female) 'birth pangs' metaphor to describe the yearning of creation for its 'glorious liberty' (8.22). After Montanism (the prophetic

---

4. See, e.g., Irenaeus, *Against Heresies*, bk. 5, ch. 20 (2), in *Ante-Nicene Fathers*, vol. 1 (Peabody, MA: Hendrikson, 1994), p. 548; Origen, *On Prayer*, esp. II.3–6, in *Origen*, ed. Rowan A. Greer (New York: Paulist Press, 1979), pp. 81–170 (84–6); and Athanasius, *Letters to Serapion on the Holy Spirit*, 1.6, 1.7, 1.19, 1.24, 1.25, 4.4, in *Letters of Athanasius on the Holy Spirit*, ed. C. R. B. Shapland (London: Epworth Press, 1951), pp. 72–8, 108–13, 125–8, 184–5. These passages are discussed in my chapter 'Why Three?', pp. 43–6, and in more detail in *God, Sexuality and the Self*, ch. 3 (which contains a lengthy analysis of the reasons for the relative neglect in the Fathers of Romans 8 as a source of trinitarian reflection).

and rigorist sectarian movement of the second century that was eventually condemned by Rome), it is not hard to see why any or all of these features could look less than attractive to developing mainstream 'orthodoxy', at least as a first basis for trinitarian reflection. The danger of ecstatic prophecy, when loosed from the primary control of an extrinsic Logos, was one matter. This had all the drawbacks of an essentially sectarian manifestation of the faith. The releasing of 'wretched women', as Hippolytus reports of early Montanists, into positions of authority and prominence, was a second.[5] But there was a third danger, with which I think the third-century theologian Origen is primarily concerned, indeed much more than he is with Montanism. This was the danger, in any form of prayer that deliberately gives away rational mastery to the Spirit, of possible confusion between loss of control to that Spirit and loss of *sexual* control.

Let me just describe to you briefly what Origen says about prayer, trinitarianism and sexuality – all together in one nexus of association – in his fascinating treatise on prayer, the *De oratione*. I shall just draw attention to the following four features of this work, especially of its open sections, from which you will see how closely related they are to the themes I have just outlined:

The work starts in Book I with (i) an insistence on the priority and primacy of the Holy Spirit in understanding the nature and purpose of prayer; and it stresses the capacity of the grace of God to take us beyond the 'worthless

---

5. See Hippolytus, *The Refutation of All Heresies* 8.12, trans. J. H. MacMahon (Edinburgh: T&T Clark, 1868), p. 325.

reasoning of mortals' to a sphere of unutterable mysteries (see 2 Corinthians 12), where 'spiritual prayer' occurs in the 'heart'. Already, then, there is the explicit willingness to allow that the Spirit – although, from the start, a 'fellow worker' with the Father and Son – escorts us to a realm beyond the normal constraints of human rationality, even though in Origen's case there is no suggestion that the Spirit finally undermines the significance of the rational sphere. (ii) Exegesis of Romans 8 is central to the argument from the start, and citations are reiterated more than once. It is through prayer, and being 'mingled with the Spirit', that we become 'partakers of the Word of God' (X.2). (iii) This form of prayer is repeatedly, and strikingly, compared to sexual intercourse and procreation. Thus, for instance, Origen writes: 'Just as it is not possible to beget children without a woman and without receiving the power that serves to beget children, so no-one may obtain ... requests ... unless he/she has prayed with such and such a disposition.' (VIII.1) The Old Testament figure of Hannah, on this view, becomes the supreme type of the pray-er who overcomes sterility through the Spirit (II.5, etc.). But finally (iv) (and this is where we see Origen putting on the brakes), an *absolute disjunction*, according to him, must be made between the sexual and procreative theme in its metaphorical force (as we would now call it), and in its normal human, physical functioning. Thus Tatiana, the woman to whom (along with a man, Ambrose) this work is addressed, can be trusted with this approach only because she is 'most manly,' and has gone beyond 'womanish things' – in the 'manner of Sarah'

(Gen. 18.11). And knowing how 'to pray as we ought' (Rom. 8.26, see II.2) is paralleled with an appropriately 'passionless', 'deliberate' and 'holy' performance of the 'mysteries of marriage', lest 'Satan rejoice over you through lack of self control'. Unsurprisingly too, then, Origen's daring treatment of Romans 8 also occasions an immediate reminder (with reference to 1 Timothy 2 and 1 Corinthians 11), that women should always wear modest apparel and cover their heads at prayer, lest their distracting presence lead to the same sort of loss of (male) sexual control. Later in the text, too, Origen advises against praying at all in a room in which sexual intercourse has taken place (XXXI.4). The intrinsic connections between (deep) trinitarian prayer and sex, it seems, are too close, but also too dangerous.

For Origen, the answer to this closeness between trinitarianism, contemplative ascent and sexuality, and the concomitant danger of a sinful confusion of the areas, must lie in allowing only advanced contemplatives ('enoptics') – those who have also shed actual physical sexual relations – into the circle of those who may safely use the erotic language of the *Song of Songs* to describe Christ's intimate mystical embrace of us.[6] Hence erotic language becomes the (finally) indispensable mode of speaking of our intimacy with God, but only at the cost of renouncing the physical or fleshly expressions of sexuality. But it is precisely here that our third

---

6. Origen makes this point emphatically in opening the prologue of his *Commentary on the Song of Songs*. See *Origen: The Song of Songs, Commentary and Homilies*, trans. R. P. Lawson (London: Longmans, Green and Co., 1957), pp. 22–3.

question presses, one to which I have no complete and ready answer, but only some speculative – and I hope creative – suggestions.

III. *Divine and human desires*. My third thesis, you will remember, is the call to rethread the strands of tradition on divine and human desires such that they are no longer set in fundamental enmity with one another, and no longer failing in their alignment. For the fatal accompaniment of such a failure of alignment, as is all too clear in Origen (amongst others), is the denigration of non-virginal woman, or indeed any humanly desirable person, as a distractor from the divine.

What has the Trinity got to do with *this*? Let me just suggest two programmatic points in closing.

The first is the hypothesis that unless we have some sense of the implications of the trinitarian God's 'proto-erotic' desire for us, then we can hardly begin to get rightly ordered our own erotic desires at the human level. Put another way, *we need to turn Freud on his head*. Instead of thinking of 'God' language as being really being about sex (Freud's reductive ploy), we need to understand sex as really about God, and about the deep desire that we feel for God – the precious clue that is woven into our existence about the final and ultimate union that we seek. And it matters in this regard – or so I submit – that the God we desire is, in Godself, a desiring trinitarian God: the Spirit who longs for our response, who searches the hearts, and takes us to the divine source (the 'Father'), transforming us Christically as we are so taken.

In this connection there is a wonderfully suggestive passage in the fifth-century pseudo-Dionysius where Dionysius speaks of this divine *ekstasis* and yearning of God for creation catching up our human yearning into itself: 'This divine yearning', he writes, 'brings ecstasy so that the lover belongs not to self but to the beloved ... This is why the great Paul, swept along by his yearning for God and seized of its ecstatic power, has these inspired words to say: "It is no longer I who live but Christ who lives in me." Paul was clearly a lover, and, as he says, he was beside himself for God.'[7]

Now it needs to be admitted that this passage of Dionysius's is not worked out explicitly in trinitarian terms. Indeed it is open to the charge of being more influenced by neo-Platonic notions of emanation and effusion than by a strictly Christian conceptuality. But I want to suggest here that it is at least capable of trinitarian glossing, according to the model provided in undeveloped form in Romans 8, previously discussed. And on this basis I suggest that we need to have a vision of trinitarian divine *ekstasis* if we are even to begin to construct an effective and alluring theology of human sexual desire that is in some sort of analogous relationship to divine desire.

Thus secondly, and lastly: if human loves are indeed made with the imprint of the divine upon them – *vestigia* of God's ways – then they too, at their best, will surely bear the trinitarian mark. Here we have to take off afresh where Augustine left us, at that crucial moment in his *De trinitate,* at the

---

7. Pseudo-Dionysius, *The Divine Names*, 4.13, in *Pseudo-Dionysius: The CompleteWorks*, trans. Colm Luibheid (London: SPCK, 1987), p. 82.

end of book VIII, when he rejects finally the analogy of 'the lover, the loved one, and the love that binds', as inadequate to the Trinity because it is bound to bodies. 'Let us tread the flesh under foot and mount up to the soul', as he puts it.[8] But sexual loves *are* of course bodily as well as 'psychic', and if they are also to be godly, then should they not themselves mirror forth the trinitarian image in some sense? And what would that involve? Surely, at the very least, a fundamental respect of each 'person' for the other, an equality of under-standing and exchange, and the mutual *ekstasis* of attending on the other's desire as distinct, *as other*. Such a vision is the *opposite* of abuse, the opposite of distanced sexual control; it is, as the French feminist Luce Irigaray has written, with uncanny insight, itself intrinsically 'trinitarian'; sexual love at its best — she avers — is not 'egological', not even a 'du-ality in closeness', but a shared transcendence of two selves toward the other, within a 'shared space, a shared breath.' 'In this relation,' she writes, 'we are at least three ... you, me, and our creation of that ecstasy of ourself in us (*de nous en nous*) prior to any child.'[9] As each goes out to the other

8. Augustine, *The Trinity* , trans. Stephen McKenna (Washington, DC, Catholic University of America Press, 2002), 8.10 (14), 266. Of course, Augustine is fully aware, as becomes all the more evident in book XV of *De trinitate*, that *all* his analogies for God-as-Trinity are inadequate, and therefore that we are finally reliant on the grace and gift of overflowing divine love to take us into participation with Godself. (At this point, at the very end of his great trinitarian work, Augustine can himself antici-pate the vision of Ps-Dionysius in an uncanny way: see my *God, Sexuality and the Self*, ch. 7, for a more extended discussion of this theme.)

9. Irigaray, 'Questions to Emmanuel Lévinas', in *The Irigaray Reader*, ed. Maragaret Whitford (Oxford: Blackwell, 1991), pp. 178–89 (at p. 180).

in mutual abandonment and attentiveness, so it becomes clear that a third is at play – the irreducibility of a 'shared transcendence'. Here, then, we might see the Holy Spirit impinging, as pure gift, on the realm of sexual exchange – alluring, transforming, purifying, and inviting it into the divine life.

But to speak thus of the trinitarian nature of sexual love at its best is a far remove from the grimy world of pornography and abuse from which Christian feminism has emerged to make its rightful protest. Unfortunately, no language of *eros* is safe from possible nefarious application; and hence the feminist hermeneutic of suspicion can never come to an end. Even these brief suggestive reflections on divine trinitarian *eros* could, I am well aware, be put to potentially dangerous and distorted applications.[10] In this regard, Origen's caution about putting the Song of Songs into the wrong hands looks less completely wrong-headed than we might have suggested earlier: maturity, balance, prayerfulness and purification from the grosser forms of erotic selfishness and sinfulness are for him preconditions for the right use of this particular sort of theological reflection. For we do indeed play with fire when we acknowledge the deep entanglement of sexual desire and desire for God. But at the same time we acknowledge a nexus of association that is ultimately *unavoidable*, and that traditions of 'mystical

---

10. The point about the *dangers* of some feminists' use of the 'erotic' as a positive and transformative category is well made in Kathleen M. Sands, 'Uses of the Thea(o)logian: Sex and Theodicy in Religious Feminism', *Journal of Feminist Studies in Religion* 8 (1992), 7–33.

theology' have continued to discourse upon over the centuries with great insight and wisdom.

So what, finally, I have been trying to lay before you, in these brief programmatic reflections on the Trinity, prayer, and sexuality, is that this potent nexus of themes is one that no serious renewed Christianity today can afford to ignore or repress; and that only the faithfulness of prayer that reveals the nexus in the first place can hope to deliver the insights we need in developing an adequately rich trinitarian theology of sexuality to confront the ecclesiastical ructions on matters of sex and gender that now so profoundly exercise us. Once again, the task is an ascetic one, demanding patience, insight and practice.

4

'DEEPENING PRACTICES':
PERSPECTIVES FROM ASCETICAL THEOLOGY
ON BELIEF AND PRACTICE,
DESIRE AND GENDER

Introduction: A Theology of 'Deepening Practices'

IN THIS CHAPTER, I SHALL TACKLE A CONNECTED AND difficult topic which has been merely latently present in the earlier essays in this volume. The matter was already raised probingly in the first essay (on the theology of desire), when I urged that any contemporary renewal of ascetic practice would have to be committed to a lengthy project of erotic purification, and thus subject to the bumps and reversals of any such life-long ethical quest. Moreover, this was a journey that could go seriously and palpably wrong, especially if attempted without due humility and proper reliance on others' assistance within the 'mystical body' of Christ. The same issue pressed again with particular force at the end of the last chapter. For there I acknowledged that a *right* understanding of the relation of sexual desire and desire for God might only be available to those who had already stayed the course of prayer and ascetic practice through many a shoal of danger and difficulty.

In short, the undertaking of ascetic 'practice' is not one that comes with instant, commodifiable effects. Fashionable as the notion of 'practice' has become in recent philosophy and anthropology (a matter for brief discussion below), it is, alas, no less subject to ethical trivialization than those more abstract philosophical trends to which it was intended as a corrective. For everything depends on how 'practices' and their attendant meaning-systems unfold through a *sustained* narrative of commitment. It follows that we may need to complexify the notion of 'practice' from that on offer in contemporary secular philosophy in order to do justice to the variety of *different* ways in which beliefs and practices are entangled with one another at different stages of an unfolding Christian life-journey. My intention here is to show that the richly coded term 'practice' may be used with a number of discernibly different evocations in the religious sphere; and also that the logical relation of beliefs and practices may shift in different circumstances and stages of a Christian's growth to spiritual maturity. Thus it is a vital part of this argument that the 'deepening' of practices, so described, allows forms of belief to emerge that could not otherwise be accessed, even though – at the outset of any Christian life of conscious commitment – it may seem that the relationship of belief and practice operates the other way around, with belief taking the primary and structuring role. It is with these complexities in the relation of beliefs and practices that this chapter will be concerned. Along the way we shall hint at how issues of desire and gender are also, and inexorably, caught in this dance between belief and practice, and how they too undergo changes *in via*.

'Practice' has become a veritable vogue word in philosophy, ethics and anthropology in the last decades.[1] It is thus tempting to use 'practice' as a kind of methodological mantra, a concept arguably now acquiring explicative overload; but such an undiscriminating use of the term may flatten distinctions that frankly need to be made *theologically*, as has already been intimated. Reformed theology has rightly stressed the 'gift' element of all practices flowing from the infusion of grace at baptism, and on this fundamental point Catholic theology also concurs. But the effect of pressing the Reformed insistence that Christian practices must always be read, paradoxically and simultaneously, *both* via the narrative of (unmerited) justification *and* via the narrative of (responsive) sanctification,[2] may actually be to iron out certain important complexities with which pre-Reformation Catholic theology struggled mightily; for here debates focused on the technical intricacies and distinctions of different manifestations of grace – 'actual' and 'habitual', 'operative' and 'cooperative' – and thus on the ways in which human responsiveness to the divine could have different *shades*, or depths, in and through a life-time of graced interaction

---

1. I have in mind here particularly the work of Bourdieu and Hadot in France, and of MacIntyre and his followers in virtue theory in the Anglophone world. Catherine Bell's wonderful study *Ritual Process, Ritual Theory* (New York: Oxford University Press, 1992) presents a sophisticated theory of ritual practice in relation to belief which owes much to Bourdieu, but is still fundamentally secular in its assumptions.

2. See John Calvin, *Institutes of the Christian Religion*, book 3, ed. John T. McNeill, trans. Ford Lewis Battles (2 vols; London: SCM Press, 1961), vols 1.535–2.1008.

with divine love.[3]

In what follows, I shall be exploring some of these different shades within the spectrum of Christian 'practices' through the lens of traditions of ascetical and mystical theology. I shall be suggesting that Christian practices of at least three different sorts (roughly corresponding to the classical distinctions between the 'purgative', 'illuminative' and 'unitive' ways) may be distinguished, and that they could be said to relate to three different *levels* of spiritual engagement. A disjunctive understanding of these levels must, however, at all costs be avoided: although the distinction between levels has important heuristic value, in the messy reality of life the levels might well not clearly supersede one another, but blend into a continuous whole. Moreover, as we shall see, the 'practices' of earlier stages are never discarded, but taken on – and taken for granted – in what follows. Only at the third 'level' that I shall describe, however, do deepened theological insights (re-minted as 'beliefs') arise that are available *only* through prolonged engagement in 'practices'. These insights could not have been gained by a merely intellectual short-cut, however sharp or brilliant. They are *founded in* 'practices', supremely in the practice of infused contemplation, being effects of a life of multiple forms of faithfulness, forging the participants by degrees into 'the image of his Son' (see Rom. 8.29). Here the apparent extrinsicism of

---

3. An approachable account of a number of vying late-medieval theologies of grace is given in Alister E. McGrath, *Iustitia Dei: A History of the Christian Doctrine of Justification* (2 vols.; Cambridge: Cambridge University Press, 1986), vol. 1, ch. 4.

earlier forms of *imitatio Christi* gives way to a more explicit and conscious participation in that life.

But it is at this same (third) level, I suggest, that even the sceptical secular outsider will be forced to acknowledge that the ostensibly anodyne term 'practice' must give way to an overt theology of *grace*. Once this is realized, the question inevitably arises, retroactively, of whether grace was not propelling the engagement in 'practices' all along. This view is readily *asserted* by the 'orthodox' believer, of course (especially the Reformed one), but is often far from evident to the observer – or even initially, perhaps, to the believer herself. In short, there is a subtle sliding scale here: one starts from 'practices' that one might be tempted to regard as entirely self-propelled, but they are joined over time by 'practices' that involve deeper and more demanding levels of response to divine grace, and which uncover by degrees the implications of our fundamental reliance on that grace as initiated in baptism. It seems that Christian 'practices' do not happen on a *flat* plane. Because my examples in this chapter will largely be taken from the history of Christian monastic and ascetical theology, both Eastern and Western, it will be instructive to compare this material with the emphasis on the Reformed doctrine of 'sanctification'. From here, we may ask in closing whether the implied theology of grace need necessarily diverge in the two cases, and if so, how.

If we turn for a moment to a much-quoted definition of 'practice' enunciated by Alasdair MacIntyre in *After Virtue*, we shall be able to make this point about the paradox of grace and 'practice' a little more explicit. MacIntyre defines 'practice' in terms specifically of 'socially established' *human* projects: it is 'cooperative *human* activity' resulting in an extension of '*human* powers to achieve excellence' and '*human* conceptions of the ends and goods involved'.[4] If we were to go straight from this definition to an examination of distinctive Christian 'practices', we would run the risk of embracing an implicitly Pelagian understanding of the undertakings involved, or, at least, an account which *side-lines* a theology of divine interaction or co-operative grace. In order to guard against this tendency, we shall here chart the progression from a level of 'practice' which *actively* (and even aggressively) demarcates itself from non-Christian alternatives, through to the apparently *passive* 'practice' of contemplation, in which an ostensibly time-wasting attentiveness is claimed to be the unimpeded receptacle of infused grace; and we shall attempt to explicate how an unfolding response to grace propels the whole. The stereotypical gender evocations of these two poles should also not escape our notice: the unexpected 'power' of the apparent 'powerlessness' of contemplation is one that female writers in the contemplative tradition have drawn attention to, often with profoundly subversive effects; yet there is still the danger of trivializing their undertakings as mere 'feminine' submissiveness. We shall return to this point a little later, for the question of the changing gender associations of these different 'levels' is highly revealing for our theological task.

---

4. Alasdair MacIntyre, *After Virtue: A Study in Moral Theory* (Notre Dame, IN: University of Notre Dame Press, 1981), p. 175, my italics.

But how can the spectrum of cooperative grace-through-practices be given fresh attractiveness for today? Its modes of expression may seem dauntingly arcane or off-puttingly elitist; it may smack of 'works righteousness', or appear relevant only to 'professional' vowed religious. In order to counter these objections at the outset I shall first look at a contemporary, humdrum example of this spectrum of beliefs and practices in operation. Then I shall turn back to more ancient traditions of ascetical theology for illumination.

'The Deep End'

The Anglican theologian W. H. Vanstone once likened the Church (specifically the Church of England) to a 'swimming pool in which all the noise comes from the shallow end'.[5] I think this ostensibly flippant remark merits some reflection: how much academic theology, and how much posturing in ecclesiastical politics, 'comes from the shallow end'? What defensive 'practices' are characteristic of that shallow end, and what are the signs that something different, and more profound (*de profundis*), is occurring? And how much patient faithfulness, how much costly formation, how much *waiting* on the divine, are required of those who hope to enunciate beliefs 'from the deep end'?

Bill Vanstone's life is a good case for reflection here: he had a brilliant, indeed unparalleledly brilliant, undergraduate

---

5. Much of the information on Vanstone's life comes from his obituary in the *Daily Telegraph*, 15 March 1999, reprinted in Trevor Beeson, ed., *Priests and Prelates: The Daily Telegraph Clerical Obituaries* (London: Continuum, 2002), pp. 214–16.

and graduate career, but chose thereafter to labour entirely unnoticed for decades in a dreary housing-estate parish in Rochdale: here was his 'practice' for most of his career. The parish was not in the sort of housing estate where there was great physical poverty, although it was the desperation and hunger of the great depression that had originally elicited Vanstone's boyhood vocation to the priesthood. Rather, it was a suburban development which manifested the more devastating spiritual poverty of a world 'come of age' – without roots, traditions, or obvious hungers of the soul. Vanstone struggled on, and his parish grew from small beginnings. He spent a good deal of time simply walking around the streets of his parish and talking to passers-by; otherwise he was visiting folk at home or was in church saying his office; he baptized, married and buried people; on Sundays he broke bread with his congregation in the Eucharist. These were his repetitive, faithful, 'practices' as a priest. But it was a period of depression for him, and it was not obvious at the time that many of his efforts were bearing fruit. During this phase of his career he was repeatedly offered attractive academic positions, but turned them all down; and when he was made an honorary canon of Manchester Cathedral he never mentioned this fact to his flock. They continued to call him plain 'Mr Vanstone'.

Later in life, however, after his first major heart attack, he wrote three short monographs into which he poured the condensed theological wisdom gleaned from his life's 'practices' in the parish. The first, *Love's Endeavour, Love's Expense*, a meditation on his work on the housing estate and its many difficulties and unexpected glories, is about the costliness of love (the costliness of Christian 'practice', we might say) when it meets no apparent response.[6] The Christian vision of love is held up before the gaze of secular indifference and goes unrecognized: 'Hidden is love's agony, love's endeavour, love's expense.' The second book (not insignificantly for our theme, for it underscores that not all 'practices' are physically *active*) is entitled *The Stature of Waiting*, and is about the progressive, albeit slow, identification of the self with the 'handing over' of Christ to his death that is so distinctive a mark of the passion narratives.[7] The third, *Farewell in Christ*, written not long before Vanstone's own death, charts his acceptance of his own mortality, but is otherwise largely given over to an extended exposition of a Christic theology of grace.[8]

These were Bill Vanstone's contributions to 'theology from the deep end'. He chose not to write them at all until he was ready to express them from that vantage point. In them, the most acute attention to the mundane (but some-

---

6. W. H. Vanstone, *Love's Endeavour, Love's Expense: The Response of Being to the Love of God* (London: Darton, Longman and Todd, 1977); published in the United States as *The Risk of Love* (New York: Oxford University Press, 1978).

7. W. H. Vanstone, *The Stature of Waiting* (London: Darton, Longman and Todd, 1982). See also his later-published visual meditations, *Icons of the Passion: A Way of the Cross* (London: Darton, Longman and Todd, 1999). Together these prove Vanstone to be one of the great modern spiritual commentators on the passion and death of Christ.

8. W. H. Vanstone, *Farewell in Christ* (London: Darton, Longman and Todd, 1997).

times tragic and sometimes glorious) stuff of parishioners' lives is elicited from his own unwavering disciplines of
Scriptural meditation, sacramental observance, and pastoral
care (disciplines which he discreetly guarded at a time when
their very usefulness was being called into question in the
church at large). But at the deep heart of the exposition, as
expressed in *The Stature of Waiting*, is the insistence on the
unitive (and Christic) 'handing over' of the self: it is this 'contemplative' heart that is seen, at the end of Vanstone's career,
to have been beating through it all along, but to have come
to full conscious appropriation only after years of painfully
purgative faithfulness to 'practices' of *hidden* efficacy.

What then does this particular life and example tell us
about the relation of beliefs and 'practices'? What it suggests, and is now to be spelled out, is that the most purified Christian 'practice' (from whence a theology 'of the
deep end' may be enunciated), is one of being 'like God [in
Christ] ... *handed over* to the world, to wait upon it, to receive its power of meaning'.[9] It is a passage into a peculiarly
active form of passivity in which the divine pressure upon
us meets not blockage but diaphanous clarification. And this
occurs – discreetly, quietly, and often even unconsciously in
the recipient – through the *long haul* of repeated 'practices'
of faithfulness.

Purgative, Illuminative and Unitive 'Practices'

Vanstone's work, as I read it, is a kind of modern-day

---

9. Vanstone, *Stature*, p. 115.

reformulation of the more ancient wisdom of ascetical theology, a theology that does not chart ascriptions of 'belief' on a flat plane, but acknowledges the complexity of belief's reformulation and personal 'appropriation' as the subject grows in spiritual stature.

What are the different levels at which 'practices' may impinge on beliefs, or *vice versa?* Traditions of 'mystical theology' within Christianity have spoken of three such stages of ascent: the 'purgative', 'illuminative' and 'unitive' ways.[10] All of these presuppose, of course, the fundamental infusion of grace in the act of baptism; but its 'unfurling', as I suggested earlier, may be perceived as occurring over time and through these three 'stages'. Although it may be a little contrived to link these stages too neatly to particular 'practices', the idea seems worthy of an exploratory rehearsal.

At the first level, that of purgation, specific, external 'practices' in virtue arise from the initial commitment to 'belief' in baptism. Much of the emphasis is on setting one's life in a direction *different* from that of the 'world'. For this reason, the rhetoric may be largely oppositional, and the 'practices' remain somewhat legalistically construed: Christian *ethike* is being established. At the second level, 'practices' start now,

---

10. I use the patristic language of 'mystical theology' in conscious contradistinction from the modern appellation of 'mysticism', which is much influenced by William James, and subject to psychologized, individualistic interpretation with a focus on fleeting high-point 'experiences'. For an excellent contemporary introduction to the ascetical tradition of 'mystical theology' in its original (and very different) sense from that of James, see Andrew Louth, *The Origins of the Christian Mystical Tradition* (2nd edn, Oxford: Oxford University Press, 2007).

inversely, to shape (or reshape) 'belief', as a form of identification with Christ begins to flower and to unsettle the
extrinsicism of the approach of the first stage. Finally, at the
third stage, more arcane theological insights become available that are *only* the prerogative of those transformed by
lengthy and painful 'practice'.

Let me spell out these distinctions in types of 'practice' a
little further by presenting some graphic examples from the
tradition that seem to fit at the different levels.

Different Levels of 'Practice': Historic Examples

Clement of Alexandria (*c.* 150–*c.* 215) provides us in the
Paedagogos ('The Instructor') with an almost perfect example of the first conception of 'practice' we have outlined. The
text is a guide for evidently privileged converts who need
now to reconsider (and discard) elements of their former
sybaritic lifestyle. Almost all of the examples of good Christian practices that Clement enjoins on us are matters to do
with not embracing the practices of the 'world', and explicitly the practices of the rich and self-indulgent. Clement
is addressing those who are trying to sort out, as baptized
people, which of the aspects of an earlier non-Christian life
can, or cannot, be deemed appropriate to Christian virtue.
He expatiates on everything from bed-coverings to earrings;
what would the 'instructor' think of hair-plucking, make-up,
body-piercing, gold jewellery, kissing your spouse in front
of the 'domestics', or appearing naked at the baths? These
matters are clearly pressing for his audience: they need to
know in precise, even legalistic, detail what will inculcate

the virtuous Christian life; and hence the extrinsicism of the commands here – the representation of Christ as instructor, teacher, and restrainer ('Bridle of colts untamed, over our wills presiding', in the words of the famous Hymn to Christ the Saviour with which the text closes).[11] Little, if anything, emerges here about practices *shaping* belief; rather, the authoritative new-found belief is used as an ethical touch-stone for distinguishing appropriate behaviour ('practice') from inappropriate.

It is particularly revealing here to note how Clement, in his initial restraining of his converts from 'pagan' activities, is also anxious to emphasize the importance of clear gender binaries: this demarcation is seemingly all part of the 'order' that the new life in baptism implies for the Christian neophyte. (A comparison with the material to be treated under the 'unitive' way will shortly be important here.) Thus Clement underscores, for instance, that 'A true gentleman must have no mark of effeminacy visible on his face, or any other part of his body. Let no blot on his manliness, then, be ever found either in his movements or habits.'[12] Women, on the other hand, should not 'smear their faces with the ensnaring devices of wily cunning' (that is, wear make-up), but be duly 'subject to their husbands', and at all costs avoid 'ogling' and 'languishing looks'.[13] The *initial* delineation of Christian from non-Christian 'practices', then, allows no unexpected

11. Clement of Alexandria, 'The Instructor' 3.12, trans. William Wilson, in *Ante-Nicene Fathers*, vol. 2 (Peabody, MA: Hendrikson, 1994), p. 295.

12. Ibid., p. 289.

13. Ibid., pp. 286, 288.

forms of gender reversal; indeed it is best for men altogether to 'turn away from the sight of women'. 'Practices' here mark Christian purity against pagan licentiousness, and any tendency to gender fluidity is firmly repudiated. Sexual desire must be carefully managed according to exacting new patterns of self-control.

But we are in rather different territory and context, I suggest, with the implicit notion of 'practice' in play in the sixth-century *Rule of Saint Benedict*, which may form a suitable example of a second level of meaning for our term. This short text, as so many commentators have justly remarked, is a document of great practical and spiritual subtlety, as suitable for young monks as for Abbots and elders; yet it contains no actual *theory* of the transformation of the monastic self, least of all in terms of 'sexuality'. As R. W. Southern has famously underlined, there *is* no 'theory of the individual' in Benedict; rather, the *Rule* simply lays out unsystematized advice for regulating a cenobitic house, with no eye to any specific charter of spiritual development.[14] Rule 7, the crucial section on the virtue of 'humility', might appear to promise such a theory of ascent: '[Jacob's] ladder . . . is our life in this world, which for the humble of heart is raised up by the Lord unto heaven. Now the sides of this ladder are our body and soul, into which sides our divine vocation has fitted various degrees of humility and discipline which we have to climb.'[15] On closer inspection, however, this is no ladder of

14. R. W. Southern, *The Making of the Middle Ages* (London: Hutchinson, 1967), p. 213.

15. *The Rule of St. Benedict*, trans. Justin McCann (London: Sheed and

logically arranged stages, and the irony of *Jacob's* ladder is that one 'descends' as easily as one 'ascends' on it. But herein lies the interesting rub for our purposes. The 'practices' of Benedict's *Rule*, ranging from psalm-singing to harvesting to welcoming strangers, all quite explicitly mapped out so that 'nothing will be [too] harsh or burdensome',[16] are no longer so much ways of keeping the 'world' at bay; but nor are they activities which will immediately (let alone invariably) produce an elevation on a scale of 'virtue'. Rather, they are to be followed in order that, *over a lifetime*, there may be an habituating of *love*, an imitation in a more than extrinsic way of the life of Christ: so that 'we shall run with unspeakable sweetness of love in the way of God's commandments; so that, never abandoning his rule but persevering in his teaching in the monastery until death, we shall share by patience in the sufferings of Christ.'[17] Here, it seems, there is the distinct suggestion that 'practice' (in this second sense) will re-modulate beliefs, will cause us to find 'Christ', for instance, in new and unexpected places — in the beggar at the door, in our own spiritual endurance and suffering, in the ministrations of the Abbot. Christ is no longer, as in Clement, the 'Instructor', reminding one, rather punitively, of one's new Christian duties; Christ does not dominate in Benedict, but is found more implicitly in postures of service.

Benedict's *Rule*, precisely in its unsystematic nature,

Ward, 1970), ch. 7, 17.

16. Ibid., prologue, 4.

17. Ibid.

makes one reflect on the almost subliminal and unconscious way in which spiritual re-modulation and transformation may occur over a life-time through repeated 'practices'. It is not obvious, for instance, why the daily and reiterated recitation in choir of psalmody should be either meritorious or life-changing ('Let nothing, therefore, be put before the Work of God'[18]): boredom might be the more predictable outcome. In practice (*sic*!) it seems that there is a kind of consciousness-expansion that unwinds in the course of this repetition; but Benedict himself nowhere expatiates on this point theoretically. It does however alert us to the importance of disciplined repetition in the fruitful interaction of belief and 'practice'. Moreover, bodily acts of worship and attention (even if the mind is distracted) have their own integrity and effect; as the anthropologist Talal Asad has remarked, unbelief can be more truly the effect of 'untaught bodies' than of uninstructed minds.[19] That Benedict gives instructions for bodies, and in particular bodies in necessarily – even uncomfortably – close interaction, is at the heart of his genius: it is through this endurance in community living, and not through virtuosity in private prayer (on which Benedict has remarkably little to say) that the 'heart' comes to be 'enlarged' 'with unspeakable sweetness of love'.[20] The enthusiasm with which 'Benedictine spirituality' has been

---

18. Ibid., ch. 43, 49.

19. Talal Asad, 'Remarks on the Anthropology of the Body', in ed. Sarah Coakley, *Religion and the Body* (Cambridge: Cambridge University Press, 1997), pp. 42–52 (at p. 48).

20. *Rule*, prologue, 4.

embraced by many non-'religious' in our generation perhaps reflects the desire for some 'bodily' integrity of this sort distinguishable from the sexualized bodiliness of Western consumer culture. Interestingly, moreover (and in strong contrast with the earlier Clement), Benedict nowhere expatiates on gender in terms, for instance, of appropriate 'manliness'. Whilst 'fraternal charity' is the goal, this is not described with the metaphors of gender stereotype, but rather with a deliberately counter-cultural stress on 'humility'. Even the section of the *Rule* on dress manages to avoid all mention of gender expectations, something that would have been unthinkable for Clement. Societal gender expectations have, it seems, been left behind in a curiously freeing way; but there is no hint, either, of any positive *upturning* or subverting of gender binaries, as we shall find in much developed 'mystical theology'.

This second, communal, interaction between 'practice' and 'belief' seen in Benedict undergoes a further twist, then – or so I submit – in a third level of engagement at which Benedict only lightly gestures (through the appeal to earlier Egyptian sources, especially via Cassian). Here I shall concentrate on that minority strand in Christian theology and spirituality which has claimed that it is possible in this life to be *incorporated* into the life of the Trinity. And with this we arrive at a specific focus of this chapter's attempted contribution – 'theological insights available *only* through practices', a contentious one granted the smack of elitism that it inevitably suggests, especially to the suspicious Protestant investigator. It is the fourth-century Evagrius of Pontus, one

of the earliest exponents of this claim, who writes: 'If you
are a theologian, you will pray truly. And if you pray truly,
you are a theologian'.[21] And (not coincidentally) it is Evagrius who also writes, 'We practise the virtues in order to
achieve contemplation of the inner essences [*logoi*] of created things, and from this we pass to contemplation of the
Logos who gives them their being; and He manifests himself
when we are in the state of prayer'.[22] Evagrius well stresses,
however, the arduous process through which 'pure prayer'
in this sense is achieved: it is no beginner's prerogative, nor
is it a possession that can be counted on to endure – the
'cunning demon' is ever out to destroy or distract. Nonetheless, sustained prayer 'practices' here are clearly the *pre-
requisites* of certain forms of theological knowledge – direct
contemplative knowledge of the Logos. How do we assess
this line of thought, apparently so differently expressed
from the gentle but untheorized assimilation to the human
life of Christ sketched in Benedict? Is it necessarily tainted
with the suspicious Platonism of Evagrius, with his distrust
of the body and his less-than-robust appreciation of community?

Since Evagrius fell under the sixth-century ban of 'Orige-
nism', his reputation is overlaid with these charges of hetero-
doxy. His mixed attitude to the body and the material world,
his doctrinal eccentricity, and his apparently individualistic

---

21. Evagrios the Solitary, 'On Prayer', in *The Philokalia,* trans. and eds
G. E. H. Palmer, Philip Sherrard and Kallistos Ware (London: Faber and
Faber, 1979), pp. 55–71 (at p. 62).

22. Ibid, pp. 61–2.

emphasis, make him an uneasy hero for one bent on explicating the doctrinally disclosive effects of 'practice' through community as well as private devotion. Yet Evagrius is one of the most significant early monastic writers to discourse on incorporation into the trinitarian life, and with that on the vital, indeed *logical*, connection between the 'practice' of 'pure prayer' and that incorporation, that re-minted understanding of 'belief'. Can this line of thought be re-expressed in less heterodox mode? The answer is surely 'yes'.

Much later, for instance, in the works of the sixteenth-century Carmelites in the West, we find a similar – indeed intensified – insistence on the lengthy and purgative process preceding the appropriation of beliefs in this mode. In the cases of Teresa of Ávila and John of the Cross, this is an explicit account of the incorporation into the life of the Trinity as a result of transforming union. But it is interesting to see how *corporeal* this transformation is in its effect. In Teresa's description (in the 'Seventh Dwelling' of the *Mansions*), union does bring an 'intellectual' understanding of the meaning of the doctrine of the Trinity, but it is an intellectual vision that is at a *new* and deeper level of response than previously known – 'in the extreme interior, in some place very deep within …'[23] It is earthed, embodied. This contrasts forcefully, and revealingly, with the account of (so-called) 'union' in the earlier *Life*, in which unitive states were brief, ecstatic, physically disabling, and not marked by

---

23. Teresa of Ávila, 'The Interior Castle' VII.1, in *The Collected Works of St. Teresa of Ávila,* trans. Kieran Kavanaugh and Otilio Rodriguez (2 vols; Washington, DC: Institute of Carmelite Studies, 1980), vol. 2, p. 430.

recognition of doctrinal content[24] — in short, 'experiences' of the sort now misleadingly termed 'mystical' in the falsely psychologized modern sense. This Teresa now eschews. The Teresa of the *Mansions* sees that it is a higher state to be able to withstand lasting union without physical ecstasy or collapse, and the acknowledgement of the trinitarian element is a concomitant feature of that more exalted position. The return to the quotidian, to 'the pots and pans' of the kitchen, is incarnationally *required* of the one who passes into this union; any flight from the 'ordinary', and thus from the continuing round of bodily 'practices' in community which mark its Christian shape, would be a denial of the very trinitarian revelation just vouchsafed. This is no flight from the material, the everyday, or the chafing realities of the 'other'. Nor is this 'union' a fleeting 'experience'; it is a permanent, incarnated, reality.

In John of the Cross's similar account of union in *The Spiritual Canticle*, the seemingly even more daring claim is made that the soul can actually breathe with the 'very breath' of the Spirit that moves between the Father and the Son; the soul is actually now knit into the life of God, its 'belief' wholly internalized by the long 'practice' of contemplation: 'And thus the soul loves God in the Holy Spirit together with the Holy Spirit, not by means of Him, as by an instrument, but together with Him, by reason of the transformation ... and He supplies that which she lacks by her

---

24. See, for instance, *The Life of St. Teresa*, trans. J. M. Cohen (London: Penguin, 1957), ch. 18.

having been transformed in love with Him'.[25]

The gender play, we note, in this third level of transformation is altogether different again from the preceding stages. Whereas in Clement the instantiation of strong gender binaries was perceived as a bulwark against pagan immorality, and in Benedict gender seemed to become almost irrelevant to the programme of subliminal community transformation, here the notable adoption of the 'feminine' posture of the soul by John, and the emergence of a strong voice of authority in Teresa (a contrast to her ostensibly self-belittling 'rhetoric of femininity' in the *Life*) illustrate the characteristic gender transformations of mystical theology's possibilities. Yet for both Teresa and John it is the *sui generis* responsiveness ('passivity' is too negatively loaded a word) of the soul before God that is the hallmark of these states, in which 'contemplation' is clearly now no *human* 'practice' at all, but the direct infusion of divine grace.

And that brings us to our final considerations.

Conclusions: Theologies of Grace

Clearly something crucial has occurred to the notion of 'practice' in thus charting different levels of appropriation and relation to 'beliefs'. At the third level, just described, an approach to the Trinity is hazarded that, it is claimed by the contemplatives concerned, can only be the epistemological preserve of those already transformed by divine

---

25. John of the Cross, 'The Spiritual Canticle', stanza 37, in *The Complete Works of John of the Cross*, trans. E. A. Peers (3 vols; London: Burns and Oates, 1965), vol. 2, p. 165.

grace itself to the point of 'spiritual marriage'. But what culminates in 'union' has throughout, as now can be more clearly seen, been sustained by God's providence; even the ostensibly trivial acts of Christian self-definition in the neophyte (such as abandoning the wearing of jewellery, one of Clement's bug-bears) have their 'graced' dimension. But it would be odd, on the view of the authors examined, to see this change in sartorial habit as *on a par* with the final state of union: each may finally lead there, but the goal is a progressive purification of the self so as to become transparent to the divine.

We have seen, then, that 'practice' may have a *variety* of meanings in the Christian context, and those meanings are significantly affected by the depth of response involved in the believer. 'Contemplation' in the Carmelites may be termed a 'practice', but strictly speaking it is done ('infused') by God in the believer: it is, from the human side, the *purest* act of willed 'passivity'. The contemplative, however, does not then give up 'practices' of more mundane sorts that have formed and shaped her in the earlier stages of 'ascent'; ostensibly trivial decisions about modest dress, or habits of hospitality to the poor, continue to be taken for granted, yet they get taken up and further transfigured. Just as a concert pianist never ceases from the mundane, and often tedious, practice of scales, so the contemplative, as Teresa shows with such genius, is thrust back into the repetitive hurly-burly of the kitchen or the market-place.[26] Even the hermit, as the

---

26. Teresa, 'Interior Castle' VII.4, 448, on the importance of Martha in conjunction with Mary.

literature of the Desert Fathers so memorably reminds us, goes back to basics day by day as he is reminded of the frailty of his endeavours.[27]

Are then the traditions of 'contemplative' ascent sketched here compatible with the Reformed reading of 'justification' and 'sanctification'? Here we have to face some hard questions in closing. Luther and Calvin of course both held Pauline-inspired views about the incorporation of the believer into the 'body of Christ': Christologically there was much continuity with pre-Reformation tradition. But whereas Calvin was to work out his ecclesiology in terms of the paradoxical relation of the two narratives of 'justification' and 'sanctification', the material we have here charted was, in its Western medieval forms, undergirded by theories of grace which distinguished *different* levels and types of grace's effects. The danger of spiritual elitism in those theories that caused nervousness (if not outright rebuke) in the reformers is hard to deny altogether in the material we have covered here. And the significant differences in *emphasis*, at least, between pre-Reformation and Reformed theories of 'justification' are not ones that can be magicked away, as the most recent *Concordat* between Rome and the Lutherans amply shows.[28] It is not my purpose here to claim

27. See, e.g., the many sayings of this type from the *Apophthegmata Patrum*, in *The Wisdom of the Desert Fathers*, trans. Benedicta Ward (Oxford: SLG Press, 1975).

28. See the 'Joint Declaration on the Doctrine of Justification' by the Lutheran World Federation and the Roman Catholic Church (available at http://www.elca.org / Who-We-Are / Our-Three-Expressions / Churchwide-Organization / Office-of-the-Presiding-Bishop / Ecu-

that these historic points of division can be erased by an eirenic smudging of them with the category of 'practice' — that would be a mere sleight of hand. If the argument of this chapter has been successful, however, a theology of 'deepening practices' may take from the insights of classic ascetical and mystical theology a message about the relation of 'practice' and 'belief' not obviously incompatible with the central instincts of the Reformers, although certainly questioning some of their rhetorical disjunctions. This position has been forwarded on the assumption (I trust sufficiently supported) that the monastic circles that spawned these traditions are not the sole preserve of their application; lay theologies of 'belief' and 'practice' are equally open to the transformative undertakings this literature proposes for body and soul, not least the vocation of a 'contemplative life'.

To sum up: a spectrum of (differently) interactive forms of 'beliefs' and 'practices' has here been suggested through which, over a life-time of faithful observation of both public acts of worship and charity on the one hand, and private devotions on the other, one might hope ultimately to come to 'know' God in God's intimate life — to breathe his very Spirit, as John of the Cross puts it. I have proceeded on the assumption that this is the vocation to which all Christians are called, and I have attempted to give clarity to an (admittedly) complex and messy entanglement of beliefs and practices by suggesting a three-stage heuristic schema of

menical-and-Inter-Religious-Relations / Bilateral-Conversations / Lutheran-Roman-Catholic / The-Joint-Declaration. aspx), which does not attempt to obliterate the differences of emphasis between Roman Catholic and Lutheran approaches.

the relation of 'belief' to 'practice'. At the first stage, when the neophyte sets out to delineate the *differentia* of Christian over secular life, it is the public, given 'beliefs' of the creeds that logically precede, and substantially inform, the initial 'practices' of Christian life; certain 'pagan' practices are forsworn. This much we saw in Clement. But a 'devout life' cannot stop with such externals, however meritorious; it engages in a whole web of interactive everyday Christian practices, such as Benedict prescribes, in which the logical relation of practices to beliefs starts to change: the two become mutually interactive. More or less subliminally, and with a loosening of previous moral judgmentalism, the 'inner' meanings of beliefs start to make their impact. 'Christ' ceases to be merely an external model to be imitated, but recognized in the poor, the stranger at the gate; creeds cease to be merely tools of judgment, but rather rules of life into which to enter and flourish; 'beliefs' cease to be merely charters of orthodoxy dictating right practice: instead (and conversely) 'practices' start to infuse 'beliefs' with richer meaning. Finally, the 'practices' of prayer that have all along sustained this process may, if the contemplatives are to be believed, be purified and simplified into silent responsiveness, into an empty waiting on God which precedes 'union' in its full sense. This 'practice' of contemplation is strictly speaking God's practice *in* one – a more unimpeded or conscious form of that distinctive human receptivity to grace which has sustained the process all along and which is itself a divine gift. But it does not obliterate or invalidate all the other practices (which continue); rather it sets them all in a new light, reversing more obviously now the logical relation of 'beliefs' and 'practices' as this 'practice' finally discloses the *incorporative* telos and meaning of 'beliefs'. In particular, the Trinity is no longer seen as an obscure, albeit authoritative, ecclesial doctrine of God's nature, but rather a life into which we enter and, in unbreakable 'union' with Christ, breathe the very Spirit of God. Such is the goal of a life animated from the start by *desire* for Christ, and accompanied by fascinating shifts in perceptions of (both worldly and unworldly) understandings of 'gender'.

Such a vision of the Christian life may still, to the Protestant, smack suspiciously of elitist progressivism, and that nettle has here been grasped. But what this vision most emphatically does *not* propound is the intrinsic spiritual superiority of any particular vocation, lay or ordained, let alone the necessity of high-point 'experiences' of the divine, which are in any case in the Carmelite tradition treated with great reserve. That is why, in closing, it is worth recalling again the witness of Bill Vanstone, who – Anglican as he was – was profoundly affected by both Calvinist and Catholic theologies of grace, and who would have thought it absurd if someone had described him as a 'mystic' in the modern, experientialist sense.[29] We should not presume, that is, in this reading of ascetical and contemplative literature, that its insights about what Vanstone called the 'deep end' are incompatible with a life of tough ordinariness, ministerial obscurity, and even a sense of human failure: '*Hidden* is love's agony, Love's endeavour, love's expense', as Vanstone reminds

29. See again my warning remarks about 'mysticism' in n. 10, above.

us. Even so, the 'deep end' has silently, and powerfully, been explored. The uncelebrated 'mystical theologian' is no less a contemplative for being uncelebrated; the transformative 'stature of waiting' (often affectively felt as 'waiting without hope', as T. S. Eliot memorably puts it in *The Four Quartets*[30]) is a profoundly counter-cultural act, a 'practice' mastered only over a life-time, which nonetheless may bear away some of the world's pain.

---

30. T. S. Eliot, 'East Coker' III, from *The Four Quartets*: 'I said to my soul, be still, and wait without hope, For hope would be hope for the wrong thing;' in *T. S. Eliot: The Complete Poems and Plays* (London: Faber and Faber, 1969), p. 180.

5

BEYOND LIBERTINISM AND REPRESSION: THE QUEST FOR A NEW ANGLICAN THEOLOGICAL ASCETICS

Introduction: Sexual Ethics in a Post-Colonial World

THIS FINAL CHAPTER STARTS FROM THE CHALLENGE of listening to those 'from the margins' in an era of increasingly violent rhetorical divisiveness on matters of sexual ethics, and of outbreaks of disturbing ecclesiastical homophobia. Its goals, however, are modest. It aims only to offer a short theological 'afterword' to the varied voices that have recently sounded from such margins[1] — many of them leading Anglican representatives from the Southern Hemisphere who in Britain and North America have previously been unheard or unheeded. It is an affecting matter to read, and listen to, such voices; and surely no-one could attend to them without realizing that a central plank of the current anti-homosexual lobby within Anglicanism has now collapsed. That is, 'homosexual orientation' is by no means limited to the preserve of the Northern Hemisphere, let alone of a privileged and supposedly 'corrupt' society

---

1. See the collected essays in Terry Brown, ed., *Other Voices, Other Worlds: The Global Church Speaks Out on Homosexuality* (London: Darton, Longman and Todd, 2006), to which this chapter was originally appended as a final section of commentary, responding to those 'other voices'.

in those climes. It is a worldwide phenomenon with many faces of cultural difference, and many and complex encoded moral dilemmas.

What credentials do I myself have to offer these reflections? I write as a systematic and philosophical theologian who, during the whole of the crescendo into the Anglican Communion's current crisis over homosexuality, lived in two cultures. My academic year was spent as a professor in North America, in the predominantly 'liberal' Episcopalian diocese of Massachusetts. I spent much time at Harvard during my office hours talking with highly intelligent gay, lesbian, bisexual and transgender students who longed to give a richly theological account of their orientation and of their place in the churches they hoped to serve. These interactions were among the most profound and moving of my priestly and academic life.[2] Meanwhile, my summers were spent back in England in the theologically much more divided diocese of Oxford, where Anglican conversations on homosexuality were noticeably more fraught and tense after the 'Jeffrey John affair'.[3] I am British, and at that time was canonically resident in the diocese of Oxford; but during

---

2. Many of these students had suffered greatly, first, in 'coming out' to conservative parents or friends, and then suffered again as a result of resisting promiscuous relationships and taking a stand on Christian principles of faithfulness.

3. A brief and fair account of these sad events (when the celibate gay priest Jeffrey John was first put forward for the episcopate and then forcibly withdrawn from candidacy), can be found in Rupert Shortt, *Rowan's Rule: The Biography of the Archbishop* (London: Hodder & Stoughton, 2008).

each year I assisted in two very different parishes: one American, suburban and affluent; one English, socially deprived and struggling. So I acknowledge that what I want to say on this subject is much affected by my recent peripatetic, even chameleon-like, ecclesiastical and academic existence. Even though I am now permanently back in the English academic and ecclesiastical context (in Cambridge and the Ely diocese), what I saw and heard in my two contrasting locations in England and America during the volatile era of the Windsor Report,[4] and what I signally did *not* hear in either (despite their contrasting theological and political presumptions), deeply informs the argument I offer here.

And for what it is worth (since it is profoundly relevant to the 'contextualization' of sexual ethics, worldwide), I also lived for nearly a year, much earlier in my life, in an extremely deprived part of Southern Africa – in Lesotho, the land-locked former British protectorate surrounded by South Africa, which remains one of the poorest countries in the world. Partly because of its extreme poverty and lack of natural resources, and the absence of large proportions of its adult male population at any one time in South Africa, where they undertake manual work in the mines and elsewhere, HIV/AIDS infection is now estimated to have reached a staggering 75% of the population in some townships, including that of Mohale's Hoek, where I worked as a

---

4. *The Windsor Report* (London: Anglican Communion Office, 2004) was a first attempt to find a way through the threatened schism within the Anglican Communion by means of a proposed 'covenant' between member churches.

volunteer student teacher in 1970. Unprotected and promiscuous heterosexual contact has undeniably been almost solely responsible for the spread of this disease, along with social instability, poverty and malnutrition, poor or non-existent education, and a desperate lack of medical resources. But this is also a culture that has traditionally not spoken openly about homosexuality – a state of affairs that, in missionary contexts especially (as I discovered way back in 1970) could easily lay it open to secretive forms of promiscuity or abuse. Lesotho is now a country threatened with the prospect of dying on its feet; it represents for me the forgotten and tragic face of the privileged world's gross mismanagement of the whole 'economy of desire'. As I have argued impenitently throughout the essays in this book, sexual desire cannot, in this or any other context, ultimately be divorced from other forms of desire (for food, wealth, power, status, peace, and finally for God) – not, at least, when 'desire' itself is reflected upon *theologically*. That moral intuition will again guide what I have to say about the hugely divisive topic of homosexuality.

Beyond 'Liberalism' and 'Biblicism'

This short chapter proceeds in a pincer movement. In this first and longer section, I reflect briefly on the current Anglican debate on homosexuality and I urge that, despite much enrichment provided by pan-Anglican perspectives, the characteristic disjunction between 'liberal' and 'biblicist' opinions still remains insufficiently disturbed, and that neither option (as currently purveyed) seems appropriately rooted in reflection on 'classic Anglicanism'. I shall thus probe beneath these categories and suggest that they hide another, more insidious and false, *modern* disjunction (as already rehearsed in the Introduction to this volume), that between 'libertinism' and 'repression'. In my latter section, I shall once again propose a move beyond this second disjunction, one that would reintroduce the category of 'asceticism' into a distinctively Anglican quest for a holy or devout life, whether 'heterosexual' or 'homosexual'. This asceticism would start from the presumption of the need, in a fallen world, to chasten and purify *all* our desires before God. This conclusion necessarily fits ill with classic theological 'liberalism'. It is a paradox of the modern history of homosexuality, I shall suggest, that only 'liberalism' (whether political or theological) has fostered the courage to enable its public and political acknowledgement in the first place, but only 'asceticism' that can provide a proper matrix for its theological representation in relation to desire for God.

Let me first look briefly at the 'liberalism' / 'biblicism' divide. Many writers[5] resist 'biblicism' in the forms of biblical *literalism* or *fundamentalism*, especially as these relate to the scattered biblical injunctions against sodomy or lesbianism. Many authors reflect deeply on the complex hermeneutical processes that form part of any attempt to relate such injunctions to contemporary life in a variety of cultural contexts. But there remains a danger of assuming that 'hermeneutics' (so-called) is somehow only the prerogative of the 'liberal'. This slippage in semantic use must be resisted firmly, since

5. I refer here especially to the other contributors to *Other Voices, Other Worlds* (see note 1).

it merely plays into the hands of the opponent. (It also does an injustice to the highly sophisticated biblical scholarship undertaken on the conservative wing of the debate.) No, any serious spiritual engagement with the authority of scripture is *necessarily* 'hermeneutical', involving a demanding process of scriptural application that in no way ensures easy resolutions with contemporary mores or 'local' practices.[6] Indeed, Anglicanism has historically had its own distinctive and classic views on the process of interpretation, especially in connection with the Holy Spirit's inspiration (a prime Calvinist emphasis) and the subtle relation to 'reason', 'tradition' and 'justice' (a prime additional Anglican emphasis).

Contemporary commentators on the homosexuality debates sometimes begin to probe back to Richard Hooker's sophisticated discussion of the relations between Scripture, tradition, reason and 'natural law' in the opening chapters of the fifth book of his *Of the Laws of Ecclesiastical Polity*.[7] But far more remains to be done to raise the current worldwide Anglican debate to the level of complexity and subtlety found in Hooker's account. Scarcely, for instance, can we

---

6. This issue is admittedly discussed quite sensitively in *The Windsor Report*, paragraphs 57–62. For a particularly measured and sophisticated development of this theme, involving both conservative and liberal exegetes, see the special issue of *The Anglican Theological Review* 93 (2011); my own commentary is to be found on pp. 111–13.

7. See bk 5, chs i–ix, in *The Works of That Learned and Judicious Divine, Mr. Richard Hooker*, ed. John Keble (3 vols; Oxford: Oxford University Press, 3rd edn, 1865), vol. 2, pp. 13–41. Note especially Hooker's opening premise, that 'So natural is the union of Religion with Justice, that we may boldly deem there is neither, where both are not' (bk 5, ch i, p. 14).

call *The Windsor Report* itself a consciously 'Hookerian' document; on the contrary, its short section on 'Scripture and Interpretation' makes no mention of Hooker and his own painful debates with more staunchly literalist opponents on the Calvinist wing, even though this narrative is quite revealing for today's *contretemps*. Nor does the Report engage with Hooker's complex understanding of 'natural law' as itself in the process of a gradual unfolding to the Church's view, and its important relation to the primary authority of Scripture.[8] Indeed, the novel ecclesiological suggestions made in the Report regarding a proposed 'covenant' between various parts of the Communion smack more of Presbyterian polity than of specifically Anglican understandings of ecclesiastical order as found in Hooker and others. In short, the pole of 'biblicism' in the current Anglican disjunction of opinion hides a multitude of deeper issues which demand careful, historically nuanced attention.

But it is not only the 'biblicist' option that is open to this kind of investigation and critique. What of the 'liberal' wing

---

8. Hooker famously puts it thus: 'What Scripture doth plainly deliver, to that the first place both of credit and obedience is due; the next whereunto is whatsoever any man can necessarily conclude by force of reason; after these, the voice of the Church succeedeth. That which the Church by her ecclesiastical authority shall probably think and define to be true or good, must in congruity of reason overrule all other inferior judgments whatsoever' (ch. viii, p. 34). At this point, Hooker has just elaborated his principle that the 'Church being a body which dieth not, hath always power, as occasion requireth, no less to ordain that which never was, than to ratify what hath been before. . . . *Laws touching matters of order are changeable*, by the power of the Church; articles concerning doctrine not so' (ch. viii, p. 33, my emphasis).

of the debate, in contrast? Just as in the ostensibly opposite case of 'biblicism', I would like here to give brief attention to certain axioms, or presumptions, that surface in its enunciation, and which manifestly require deeper *theological* analysis.

Political 'liberalism' and theological 'liberalism' are by no means the same thing, and their European and American forms are also importantly different from one another.[9] Nevertheless, political and theological forms of 'liberalism' do share some presumptions and historical roots, and are often inextricably entangled, especially in the United States. To most Americans who have gone through the American public education system, the Bill of Rights seems as 'natural' as one's mother's milk — so natural, in fact, as to require no explanation or defence at all in church circles, let alone a probing of its religious underpinnings. And herein lies so much of the difficulty in the current dispute in the Anglican Communion: to so many on the political 'left' amongst American Episcopalians, the proper approach to homosexuality is simply a matter of 'rights', 'liberty', 'justice' and the 'pursuit of happiness', and there seems no need to complicate it with a discussion of arcane biblical proscriptions. Add to that a historic grudge against the original 'colonialism' of Britain and its state church, and you have the potent mix of resentments that fires the current transatlantic dispute.

---

9. It is instructive here, for instance, to compare the political and religious 'liberalism' of John Locke (as closely correlated to the Church/state arrangements in England), with the religious 'liberalism' of Thomas Jefferson in America.

However, not only in the United States does the language of political 'liberalism' dominate the ecclesiastical dispute about homosexuality. Several characteristically 'liberal' proposals and lines of argument employed even by the diverse and international authors in *Other Voices, Other Worlds* must here be identified and held up for critical consideration:

a. Sex is 'private' and not a matter for prurient intervention by Church or state; as long as no abuse is involved, and sex is 'consensual', it should be of no 'public' concern.

b. Everyone has a 'right' to 'happiness', including the happiness of sexual expression and pleasure. (A subtext here tends to be that celibacy is presumed impossible, except for a tiny minority of people with an unusual 'vocation' to it.)

c. 'Tolerance' and 'acceptance' of various different forms of sexual practice should be promoted, even demanded, in a 'liberal' society.

d. There are many more terrible ills of 'injustice' going on in the world (economic debt, poverty, war, ecological disaster) than those to do with sexuality, and because sex is 'private' and (mostly) 'harmless' we should do better to focus our ecclesiastical energies on those more pressing topics.

Perhaps we may also add to this list two other 'liberal' lines of argument, which are arguably more the product of 'post-modern' mores than of classic 'modern' thinking:

e. First, statistics show that divorces are increasing, and it is important that the church show compassion and understanding to those who cannot find happiness with the same person throughout a long life. If the Church is 'accepting' of divorced folk, it certainly should be also of homosexuals, bisexuals and transgendered people.

f. The infinite variability of sexual mores and gender roles found in many parts of the world suggests that no single standard of sexual uprightness can be imposed worldwide. Indeed, it would be imperialist to try to do so. We should support a non-coercive plurality of models for sexual expression in different cultural contexts.

What I want to note, again from a theological perspective, is that none of these arguments – *as stated* – is overtly Christian, let alone explicitly 'Anglican'.[10] Some of them do indeed have a Christian or Jewish ancestry of deep importance, but this is buried beneath an Enlightenment form of expression and it requires excavation. Others seem more questionably Christian, particularly the appeal to the supposed 'privacy' of sexuality, with the accompanying presumption that sexual expression does not affect anyone except the partners themselves. To be fair, I have isolated these 'liberal' strands of argument here in a sort of typological caricature, and many of the contributors to *Other Voices, Other Worlds* do indeed attempt theological excavation of some profundity, conjoining one or more of the strands with rich appeals to scripture,

---

10. There is insufficient space here to develop this line of argument systematically; but suffice it to say that, with the possible exception of axiom *c*, I myself subscribe to none of the 'liberal' views here formulated. Proposition *f* demands close critical attention because it slides from 'contexualization' to actual moral *relativism* (i.e., the view that 'what is moral *is* moral relative to, and in virtue of, a particular context'). It is possible, I would argue, to be extremely sensitive to the variables of context, culture, and local expectation and still maintain a non-relativistic ethic. Once again, questions of 'hermeneutical' application become all-important.

tradition and experience. But my point is merely this: to the extent that these 'liberal' arguments remain *unexamined*, *uncriticized*, and *unconnected* to the hard, Hookerian task of conjoining obedience to scriptural authority with a consideration of the inheritance of ecclesial tradition, and a close examination of the ways that 'reason', 'natural law', 'common sense' and 'wisdom' now seem to point the way forward afresh, then the task is unfinished. The argument is not yet 'Anglican'.

So far, I have been attempting to show that the polarized wings of Anglicanism that most commonly attract attention in the press and public are, at best, only residually 'Anglican' in their theological method. At one end of the spectrum is an extreme biblical fundamentalism which was very far from the ethos of the great English Reformers, and explicitly renounced by Hooker. At the other end is an American political liberalism which, though ultimately founded on religious insights, is also not Anglican in any obvious historic sense. To put it provocatively: the current 'Anglican' homosexuality debates are not Anglican at all! This is a bold claim and cannot be spelled out further historically within the constraints of this particular volume; but the claim is being made here to draw attention to the need for varied voices — which so interestingly complicate and enrich the discussion — to be heard in an authentically *theological* auditorium of reinvigorated Anglicanism. And not only that. My further hypothesis is that, beneath the regrettable churchly divide between 'biblicists' and 'liberals', which I have briefly here discussed, lies that more profound, and sometimes occluded, *worldly* divide between 'repression' and 'libertinism' which (underlyingly and falsely) fuels the passion of the debate. For it is not for nothing that 'biblicists' are often accused of enforcing sexual 'repression', and 'liberals' of encouraging sexual 'libertinism'. These categories are modern, psychoanalytic and political, lurking under the veneer of ecclesiastical debate. But, as has been repeatedly urged in the essays in this book, they always also demand our *theological* attention and critique.

Beyond 'Libertinism' and 'Repression'?

Amidst all the furores caused by churchly rows on homosexuality, not enough attention is drawn to the completely novel phenomenon of our generation – a 'new thing' in the best, Isaianic sense. That some gay and lesbian couples now wish to enter into public, and publicly accountable, lifelong vows of fidelity is, I submit, the true moral achievement of this painful cultural and ecclesiastical transition.[11] Such 'witness'[12] is indeed a demanding ascetic undertaking, and it

11. I choose not to enter here into the (to my mind, somewhat fruitless) question of whether gay and lesbian alliances should be called 'marriage'. This question of terms has legal and tax implications, of course; but since 'marriage' has, in any case, become so debased in its meaning in secular culture (often involving no serious commitment to fidelity), I would propose that 'lifelong vows of fidelity' is a better expression theologically, and avoids the issue of whether we can, or should, call heterosexual and homosexual 'marriages' 'the same' in all particulars, especially as regards procreation.

12. The Orthodox tradition of thinking of marriage as a 'martyrdom' may sound grim to contemporary Western (and Romantic) ears, but seems to me to encode some profound theological insight. Marriage is

does not only cut against the grain of remaining cultural and churchly disapproval of homosexuality itself. Perhaps more significantly, such witness is also consciously resistant to the widespread collapse of bonds of faithfulness in society at large. In this sense, and as I already urged in ch. 1 of this book, we might see the current ecclesiastical furores about same-sex desire (whether Protestant or Roman Catholic) as being not finally about 'homosexuality' or failed celibacy *per se* (although these attract the scandal-mongering) but as about a deeper crisis in the workings and siftings of desire, *tout court*. Seen in such theological terms as these, the current crisis is about the failure, in this Web-induced culture of instantly commodified desire, to submit all our desires to the test of divine longing. For the key issue in the ascetic 'training of desire', as I have stressed throughout the chapters in this book, is a lifelong commitment to personal, erotic transformation, and thereby of reflection on the final significance of all our desires before God. Such an insight applies just as significantly to the issue of homosexual desire as it does to any other form of desire. Yet this particular perspective remains profoundly countercultural, calling into question many of the 'liberal' presumptions stated earlier. Is sex 'private'? Is the 'right' to various pleasures superseded by the call to fidelity? Is my desire for wealth at the cost of Africa's ravaging ultimately disconnected from my assessment and testing of other desires, including sexual desires, before

---

indeed both a public 'witness' (*martyr*) and also, inevitably, the commitment to some forms of loss, suffering and transformation in relation and adjustment to the 'other'. Both these modes of 'witness'/martyrdom may of course be christologically conceived.

God? Thus to bind all one's desires 'into a tether' is to move out beyond the false secular disjunction between 'libertinism' and 'repression', which is based on the presumption that freedom is found only by throwing off constraint. It is, in contrast, to re-glimpse a vision of 'freedom' obtained precisely by specific, freelychosen ascetic *narrowings* of choice, fuelled by prioritizing the love of God.[13]

But herein lies our final paradox, at which I hinted in opening. For gay men and women to find even minimal acknowledgement and support in the Anglican Church, years of painful and courageous activism have been necessary. Arguably, only a 'liberal' political agenda could have sustained such activism; and the battle is certainly not yet over. The quest for 'liberation', 'acknowledgement' and 'justice' is hard enough to maintain in the current climate. The ascetic quest for holiness, *conversatio morum*,[14] fidelity, and certain forms of consciously chosen constraints of desire, may seem to sit uneasily, even oppressively, alongside such a quest. But just as the battle between 'biblicism' and 'liberalism' in the Anglican homosexuality-wars is forcing Anglicans back into

13. Note again that this approach makes 'life-vows' in heterosexual and homosexual partnerships curiously similar to monastic vows of celibacy, and notably different from a careless or faithless approach to 'marriage'. As suggested by the views and example of Gregory of Nyssa discussed in ch. 1, above, the close relationship of vows of celibacy and of faithful sexual partnership are worth re-thinking in today's secular climate of sexual hedonism and infidelity.

14. This is the Benedictine vow of 'conversion of life', which – along with the correlative vows of 'obedience' and 'stability' – form the bedrock of Benedict's vision of the monastic venture. For more on the significance of continual reform in virtue in the Benedictine vision, see ch. 4, above.

a deeper reconsideration of their theological heritage in order to re-mint it for today, so here, too, the witness of gay couples, choosing to make public vows (and thus cutting not once, but twice, against cultural expectation), demands of us all a deeper reconsideration of the meaning, and costliness, of such vows in a world of rampantly promiscuous desires, the oppression of the poor, and the profligate destruction of natural resources. Seen thus, I suggest, one can no longer respond, in classic 'liberal' mode, 'Can we talk about something else? The poor are dying and the oppressed are suffering, and *you are obsessing about sex?*' No, we must give attention to all the other ways in which our many and competing desires may be at odds with God's. In sum, the task for the Anglican Communion today is, at its deepest level, theological and spiritual: not merely to reconsider its subtle and distinctive heritage regarding scripture, tradition and 'reason', but to re-enliven its demanding vision of the 'devout life'.

ACKNOWLEDGEMENTS

Permission to reprint the essays in this book (now lightly revised) is gratefully acknowledged to the following publishers, journals and editors:

Ch. 1 originally appeared as 'Pleasure Principles: Toward a Contemporary Theology of Desire', *Harvard Divinity Bulletin* 33, 2, (2005), 20–33. It is reprinted with thanks to the editors of the *Harvard Divinity Bulletin*.

Ch. 2 originally appeared as 'The Woman at the Altar: Cosmological Disturbance or Gender Fluidity?', *Anglican Theological Review* 86 (2004), 75–93. It is reprinted with thanks to the editors of the *Anglican Theological Review*.

Ch. 3 originally appeared as 'Living into the Mystery of the Holy Trinity: Trinity, Prayer, and Sexuality', *Anglican Theological Review* 80 (1998), 223–32. This is also reprinted with thanks to the editors of the *Anglican Theological Review*.

Ch. 4 originally appeared as 'Deepening "Practices": Perspectives from Ascetical and Mystical Theology', in eds Miroslav Volf and Dorothy C. Bass, *Practicing Theology: Beliefs and Practices in Christian Life* (Grand Rapids, MI: Eerdmans, 2001), pp. 78–93. It is reprinted with thanks to the senior editors of Wm. B. Eerdmans Publishing Company, Grand Rapids, Michigan, all rights reserved.

Ch. 5 originally appeared as 'Beyond Libertarianism and Repression: The Quest for an Anglican Theological Ascetics', in ed. Terry Brown, *Other Voices, Other Worlds: The Global*

Church Speaks Out on Homosexuality (London: Darton, Longman and Todd, 2006), pp. 331–8. It is reprinted with thanks to the senior editors of Darton, Longman and Todd (UK) and Church Publishing Incorporated (USA), all rights reserved.

INDEX

agape, 45-47, 52

Alcoholics Anonymous, 25

Anglicanism, 26-27, 31, 33-34, 36, 60-61, 126, 129-143

arianism, 29

Armstrong, Karen, 25

Asad, Talal, 116

ascent, 42, 44-45, 95, 111, 114, 122-3

ascetical theology, 7, 33, 101, 105, 107, 111

asceticism, 1-28, 133

Athanasius, 92

Augustine of Hippo, 30, 49, 97-8

Basil of Caesarea, 29, 51

Bates, Stephen, 31

Bell, Catherine, 79, 103

Bell, Daniel, 32

Benedict of Nursia, 19, 114-118, 121, 125, 142

Berry, Jason, 31

biblical fundamentalism, 133, 139

biblicism, 132-133, 135-136, 142

Bishop, Jeffrey, 21

body, 1-2, 7, 15, 23-27, 29, 60, 71, 92, 101, 112-118, 123-124

Bourdieu, Pierre, 79, 103

Brooks, David, 38

Brown, Peter, 15

Brown, Terry, 129

Burrus, Viriginia, 17

Butler, Judith, 82

Cadenhead, Raphael, 7

Calvin, Jean, 103, 123, 126, 134-135

Cassian, John, 19, 24, 117

celibacy, 29-31, 34-36, 38-40, 44-52, 137, 141-142

Clark, Elizabeth A., 17

Clark, Gillian, 17

Clement of Alexandria, 112-113, 115, 117, 121-122, 125

Coakley, Sarah, 1-2, 59, 66, 85, 116

colonialism, 129, 136

conservativism, 26, 32, 35-36, 55, 57-58, 62, 64, 68, 76, 81, 130, 134,

contemplation, 104, 106, 118, 120-122, 125

control, 1, 9, 11-12, 20-23, 36, 49, 86, 92-95, 98, 114

Cornwell, John, 25

Cox Miller, Patricia, 17

Crammer, Corinne, 69